THE METACULTURAL THEATER OF OH T'AE-SŎK

THE
METACULTURAL
THEATER
OF OH T'AE-SŎK

Five Plays from the Korean Avant-Garde

TRANSLATED BY

Ah-jeong Kim and R. B. Graves

UNIVERSITY OF HAWAI'I PRESS

Honolulu

Printed in the United States of America
04 03 02 01 00 99   5 4 3 2 1

Library of Congress Cataloging-in-Publication Data

O T'ae-sŏk, 1940–
The metacultural theater of Oh T'ae-sŏk : five plays from the
Korean avant-garde / translated by Ah-jeong Kim and R.B. Graves.
p.   cm.
Includes bibliographical references.
Partial Contents: Bicycle — Intimacy between father and son — Ch'un-p'ung's wife
— Lifecord — Why did Shim Ch'ŏng plunge into the sea twice?
ISBN 0-8248-2099-1 (cloth : alk. paper). — ISBN 0-8248-2158-0
(pbk. : alk. paper)
I. Title.
PL992.58.T28A24   1999
895.7'24—dc21   98-51873
CIP

University of Hawai'i Press books are printed on acid-free paper and meet the guidelines for permanence and durability of the Council on Library Resources.

This book has been published with the aid of a grant from the Daesan Foundation.

Designed by Trina Stahl
Printed by Thomson-Shore, Inc.

CONTENTS

PREFACE

OFFERED HERE ARE the first English translations of five plays by Oh T'ae-sŏk, Korea's most gifted playwright and one of the most original dramatists and directors working in Asia today. Although these translations attempt to be as accurate as possible, we have felt an equal obligation to make them playable for English-speaking actors and audiences. Compromises between cultural fidelity and dramatic practicality have been inescapable, but the drama of a man so dedicated to exploring the dialectics of Korean culture and living theater makes such give-and-take inevitable, even desirable.

A more specific problem for translators of these plays resides in the nature of the Korean texts. As a working dramatist and director, Oh T'ae-sŏk regularly makes changes, usually minor but occasionally significant, in his first written versions as he progresses through rehearsals, performances, and revivals of his plays. The published Korean texts do not always reflect these changes. In general we have translated the latest available text, although in a few instances we have included material from earlier drafts because they sometimes made uniquely Korean ideas more explicit. Many of the changes Oh introduces in rehearsal involve his use of stunning stage imagery, and even the most complete Korean texts rarely indicate the full extent of the nonverbal elements in his productions. At his urging, we have occasionally added stage directions describing the mise en scène of performances we have seen when their inclusion seemed essential to understanding the action on stage.

An earlier version of *Intimacy between Father and Son*, as translated by Ah-jeong Kim, appeared in *Asian Theatre Journal*, and we thank its editors for permission to print our considerably revised version here.

The translators would also like to thank the Daesan Foundation of Seoul, Korea, for its generous support of this project and, above all, Oh T'ae-sŏk for his enthusiastic help and cooperation.

INTRODUCTION

KOREA'S LEADING PLAYWRIGHT, Oh T'ae-sŏk has contributed an impressive collection of over thirty plays to the growing repertoire of theater pieces that attempt to mediate between Korea's native cultural heritage and contemporary Western dramatic modes. He is a committed avant-gardist who mines Korea's cultural and theatrical traditions, not so much to preserve them as to interrogate them in the light of contemporary social conditions and post-Artaudian aesthetics. His recent plays are highly original and often disturbing explorations of his country in the context of several cultures—ancient and modern, Eastern and Western—which have both nourished and ravished it.

Without formal education in theater, Oh T'ae-sŏk emerged in the late 1960s as a prominent opponent of theatrical realism, which had for many years been imported from Europe, Japan, and America and modified into a form that Korean critics labeled *shin-gŭk* (new play). Oh associated himself with various theater groups that sedulously introduced European and American nonrealistic and absurdist drama to Korea, and his plays from the late 1960s— *A Change of Season* and *Judas, Before the Rooster Crows,* in particular—bear a vague resemblance to the Harold Pinter of *Old Times* (1970), wherein young married couples in contemporary urban settings are tormented by their memories of former lovers and are stranded in an irredeemable past.

It was in preparing an adaptation of Molière's *Les Fourberies de Scapin* in 1972, however, that Oh began to investigate the possibilities of merging Western and indigenous Korean theatrical conventions. He saw that the pervasive influence of the Italian commedia dell'arte in the play could successfully be rendered by transposing this seventeenth-century French comedy into the framework of the traditional Korean form of theater known as *madang kŭk* (literally, field or outdoor play, a generic term for traditional masked dance-theater) with its own typed characters, loose plot lines, and raucous improvisation. At the same time, Oh realized that there were fundamental differences between the two theater forms, not the least of which was what he calls the "poetic rhythms of indigenous Korean narrative." In search of these rhythms, Oh undertook an expedition into Korea's mythological and historical past, not to collect artefacts, as it were, but to participate in contemporary Korea's ongoing dialogue with its cultural inheritance.

This expedition began with his play *Grass Tomb* (Ch'obun), which employs a disturbing leitmotif drawn from an ancient Korean funeral custom of burial in a grass tomb. Under the direction of Yu Tŏk-hyŏng, the play premiered in Seoul in 1973 and elicited controversy unprecedented in the history of modern Korean theater, largely due to what was seen as its jarring mixture of Western-inspired surrealism and native dramatic materials. In the following year, *Grass Tomb* became the first Korean play to be introduced to the professional English-speaking theater, when Yu directed a revival featuring American actors under the title *Jilsa* (The Order) at La Mama, the Experimental Theater Club, in New York City.

In preparation for the American production, Yu held a three-month workshop with Western actors, teaching them the body movements of Korea's traditional martial arts. Whereas in Korea he had focused on creating visual images without paying particular attention to indigenous Korean costumes or motifs, Yu now dressed the actors in traditional Korean clothes, left untranslatable Korean words in Korean, and asked the American actors to recite them as incantations. At La Mama the play evolved into a highly ritualistic presentation, and Peter Brook, who attended both the workshop and the performance, concluded that "it successfully showed a direction for which new theater was looking." Although the production was critically acclaimed, Oh T'ae-sŏk gained little recognition in the United States, and he continues to be largely unknown to the English-speaking world.

For subsequent plays, Oh has delved ever deeper into Korean history in search of what he calls a Korean ethos. In this attempt to investigate "Koreanness," Oh borrows dramatic themes from both premodern and contemporary history; three of the plays translated here—*Bicycle, Intimacy between Father and Son,* and *Lifecord*—are based directly on historical incidents, but from widely different time periods. Oh views Korean history as both the result and the cause of the collective memory and spirit of the Korean people, and if it is true that they are in danger of losing a native spirituality as a result of Western cultural influences, Oh believes that such spirituality can be revived not simply by cherishing tradition but by confronting its relationship to the present and to Western culture.

It is Oh T'ae-sŏk's view that Korean history is essentially tragic. In the space of a century, the Korean people have experienced the collapse of the five-hundred-year-old Chosŏn dynasty, Japanese occupation, the Korean War, the division of the country, military dictatorship, and widespread social unrest. These events have affected the lives of virtually every Korean, and Oh's own life provides a representative example. Born in 1940, five years before Korea's liberation from Japanese colonialism, he lost his father and two of his uncles during the Korean War ten years later. But because the war claimed the lives of nearly 2.7 million people, his experience is not simply "personal." In a country where collectivism is an official ideology, the Korean people have suffered—and ultimately created—their history together. In this context, Oh hopes to reify history through theater. In a 1992 interview with *Asahi Shimbun,* a leading Japanese newspaper, Oh explained his interest in historical themes: "Japanese colonial rule, the division of the country into south and north, the clash between the government and students . . . in every respect, Korea is a tragic country. And the reason lies in the history. When you feel provoked at what you see on stage, you are reading our history."

IN 1983, Oh T'ae-sŏk explored the Korean War and the scars it left behind in his play *Bicycle*, which premiered in 1983 at the Korean Theater Festival under the direction of Kim U-ok. Oh T'ae-sŏk later restaged the play in Seoul in 1987 and has subsequently directed nearly all of his plays for the Mokhwa Repertory Company. *Bicycle* (Chajŏngŏ) is based on an incident that took place in a southern Korean village named Sŏch'ŏn, which happens to be Oh T'ae-sŏk's hometown. Indeed, several of the minor characters in the play are based on distant relatives of the playwright. In September 1950 North Korean troops, during a brief occupation, arrested 127 anticommunists and locked them up in the town registry building. Realizing that they could not take these prisoners with them when they retreated, the North Korean soldiers burnt down the registry building with all 127 people inside. In dramatizing this atrocity, Oh T'ae-sŏk approaches his subject obliquely by adopting a dramatic technique similar to the "stream of consciousness" employed by such writers as James Joyce and Virginia Woolf. Oh introduces a township clerk named Yun as his leading character, and the story unfolds through Yun's recollection of the past mingled with his experiences in the present. Lacking a logical or chronological sequence, the play simply follows his troubled meditations on the war and its aftermath.

The play begins when Yun and his colleague Ku are returning home from work at nightfall. Yun commutes by bicycle, providing a vital metaphor for the play, because, as the bicycle rolls back and forth between his office and home, Yun's story spins out its meaning as a negotiation between past and present. It transpires that Yun recently had a mysterious encounter with a ghost and has been ill for forty days. He tells Ku of his reflections during this illness, which constitute fleeting glimpses of the town's history. Yun's mysterious experiences started on the night he and his family held a memorial service for his father, who died in the fire. Indeed, on that same night, most of the households in town were performing similar memorial rituals for their late family members, because, we learn, it is the thirtieth anniversary of the day upon which the North Koreans ordered villagers to set fire to the registry office building, thus killing all the people inside. Yun's response to these services is perhaps even more immediate than that of other towns-people, because his own uncle was one of the villagers ordered to set the registry ablaze. Every year, in fact, Yun must watch as his uncle, in a personal ritual that runs parallel to his family's public memorial service, cuts his own face with a piece of glass out of remorse and guilt for his complicity in the massacre.

Intertwined with the story of Yun's family is a subplot about a couple afflicted with leprosy. Because they feared that their illness would pass on to their children, they gave up their children to another family for adoption. But the eldest daughter and her younger sister have discovered that they are the offspring of leprotic parents, and they not only live in fear of contracting the disease but also view their parents' illness as a familial curse. The elder sister sends her sister away to the city where no one will know her past. She is later found near the town graveyard, having failed to complete the journey to the big city.

In the structure of the play, the story of Yun's family represents the grim history of the Korean War (the past), while the story of the house of lepers represents Korea's legacy (the present) in the symbolic form of a disease. The two seemingly unrelated plots are connected by metaphors of fire and darkness. Thus, past and present coalesce at the end of the play when the elder sister of the leprotic family burns down the house where her biological parents live in the mad hope that the disease and its curse can be ended. As the flames soar, the daughter cries out to her dead mother for forgiveness, but instead of her mother's blessing, we hear the voice of a North Korean soldier intoning the names of villagers killed in the registry fire thirty years before. After finishing the list, the voice orders Yun's uncle to set the building on fire, and he responds by cutting his own forehead. Past and present join in an act of penitential sacrifice.

In between the two plots, Oh inserts episodic tales—reminiscent of traditional Korean ghost stories—that illustrate the power of the past to haunt the future. As Yun rolls his bicycle along narrow country roads at night, he meets the ghost of an old resident who died in another fire during the war; a grandfather who drowned himself while, like Yun, he was traveling back home in darkness on his bicycle; a villager who fell into a traditional-style outhouse in the dark; another villager who, as North Korean soldiers retreated, rode into town on a bicycle to which he had attached Korean flags; and a cow that broke out of his pen at night, causing the villagers to run wild. Thus, the darkness of the present is bleakly illuminated by the conflagrations of history.

Although the diverse theatrical, historical, and social sources of the play are kept more or less distinct from each other, they nevertheless distort one another, modifying our view of them and the meaning of culture itself. In juxtaposing these various elements, Oh seeks to create a metacultural theater where cultures do not simply intersect but, rather, comment critically on each other as cultures. In *Bicycle*, the cultures of the West, Japan, ancient and modern Korea, and North and South Korea speak in different voices, but with an eloquence that transcends the particular even as it assails the universal.

OH HAS SAID that he was introduced to the special character of Korean cultural history in grade school when he was taught the story of Tanjong, fourth king of the Chosŏn dynasty, which later served as the subject of his 1974 play, *Lifecord* (T'ae). In 1456, when Tanjong's uncle, Sejo, usurped his throne, six loyal subjects attempted to restore the fifteen-year-old Tanjong. These six were scholars of a royal academy established in 1420 by Great King Sejong, grandfather of Tanjong. The six were executed for their revolt against Sejo but, according to accepted social conventions, so was each scholar's immediate family, as well as the extended families on their fathers', mothers', and wives' sides. During a discussion at the 1991 International Theater Forum in Seoul, Oh related this idea of history to his own experience:

> I encountered the concept of history for the first time when I was in fourth or fifth grade. I was taught that "A group of royal subjects died," and that if my uncle has committed a crime and has to die, it means that I must also die. I was taught that in Korea we had "to destroy three families: one's father's side, mother's side, and wife's side." I wondered, why I should die for my relative's crime? And I thought that this world was a very scary place. Later I learned that "God died for you, therefore, you should worship Him," but I have never understood this. After a while—I was born in 1940, by the way—people said, "Your country is not yours, it is taken by Japan, it is violated by Japanese people." These ideas of death, infringement, and humiliation have made me consider history in a new light. During the Korean War, my father and his two younger brothers all died, either kidnapped or unaccounted for, which is the same as being killed. What we see in the history of Korea is a series of deaths of people like An Chung-gǔn and Yun Pong-gil [leaders of the independence movement killed during Japanese rule]. I thought that this world grows by eating up its youth.

Unlike *Bicycle*, which resonates between narratives of past and present, *Lifecord* remains rooted in the fifteenth century even while it indirectly comments on the modern world. Thus Sejo's atrocities are not explicitly compared to twentieth-century events, but instead are contrasted with his former behavior as a model prince. When Sejo orders the death of a pregnant woman, for example, her grandfather reminds him that he once saved an innocent young woman from vicious sailors. By avoiding the expected storytelling of historical drama and by adopting the shocking imagery and kaleidoscopic structure of the contemporary experimental play, the play ruthlessly interrogates the old chronicles and holds up their explicit and implicit social values for reformulation.

Although infused with the language and details of medieval Korea, both *Lifecord* and Oh's next play, *Intimacy between Father and Son*, impress Korean critics as "antihistorical" dramas.

INTIMACY BETWEEN FATHER AND SON is based on yet another tragic monarch of Korea's past, King Yŏngjo, who ruled from 1724 to 1776 as the twenty-first king of the Chosŏn dynasty. One of Korea's most celebrated rulers, Yŏngjo aspired to becoming a sagacious king by adhering strictly to Confucian ideals. Yet he violated the most fundamental principles of Confucian humanism by killing his only son when, on 4 July 1762, Yŏngjo confined him in a rice chest, where he suffocated. The Korean title, *Pujayuch'in*, is a famous Confucian maxim meaning "There should be intimacy between father and son." Intimacy, however, is precisely what is lacking in the relationship between Yŏngjo and his son. Giving the play a Confucian maxim as its title is, in fact, Oh T'ae-sŏk's ironic jab at Yŏngjo, whose obsession with Confucian ideals blinds him to how far short of these ideals he falls.

Writing for a Korean audience versed in the traditional chronicles, Oh can omit or only vaguely allude to certain famous incidents, which a non-Korean audience needs to know. Yŏngjo has groomed Crown Prince Seja from birth to become a great king who will also live and rule by Confucian principles. Although the prince was obedient to his father as a boy, as he grew into adolescence he neglected his studies. The prince gradually developed a mysterious mental disorder called "clothing disease," which made him unable to wear royal regalia and ultimately led to violence. By the time of his death, the prince had murdered nearly a hundred people and, almost as bad, had become sexually promiscuous. Yŏngjo faced an agonizing conflict between his fatherly affection for his son and his duty to the kingdom and its people. As the prince's murders and lechery increased, the king finally ordered the death of his own son.

The method of the prince's execution—suffocation in a rice

chest—requires some explanation. It was a Korean tradition that when members of the royal family had to be executed, they be killed without mutilation of their bodies. Thus the conventional means of royal execution was a cup of poison. But even this method was unacceptable to Yŏngjo because he did not wish to sully his reputation by going down in history as a Confucian king who nevertheless killed his son. From Yŏngjo's point of view, the best solution was for the prince to commit suicide, and, at his father's command, the prince attempted to strangle himself several times—but in vain. Finally the king ordered that a large rice chest be produced and ordered the prince to walk into it "voluntarily." In this way, Yŏngjo hoped to exculpate himself of the crime of filicide. After eight days of confinement, the prince died and Yŏngjo issued a decree ordering that his late son be remembered as "the prince of mournful thoughts."

This saga has long captured the Korean imagination. Time and again, the story has provided outré plots for film, television, and radio melodramas. But rather than emphasizing court intrigue and medieval color, Oh focuses on the personal relationship between Yŏngjo and Seja during the final three years of the prince's life. He begins immediately after Yŏngjo has married a very young wife—a marriage to which Prince Seja objects. Although it is only briefly referred to in the play, a shadow has already been cast on Seja's life by the deaths, in rapid succession, of his principal protectors from Yŏngjo's wrath—Seja's grandmother, Queen Dowager In-wŏn, and his stepmother, Queen Chŏng-song. With their deaths, Seja lost political ground at court and his human relationships deteriorated. In the play, a royal official also announces the death of a royal minister, Min Paek-sam, only a few days after the death of another minister, Yi Ch'ŏn-bo. The causes of their deaths are unknown, but rumor had it that both were self-inflicted because these ministers felt responsible for Seja's madness and misdeeds. Seja seemed to have grieved genuinely over the death of his stepmother. Even after the nation's three-year period of mourning, the prince conducted private memorial rites involving elaborate funeral robes and weapons to ward off evil spirits at her shrine. Still, Yŏngjo viewed Seja's veneration of his stepmother with suspicion, misconstruing his son's private rituals as surreptitious preparations for patricide.

The role of Seja's biological mother, Lady Sŏn-hŭi, in all of this is not always clear in the ancient records, perhaps because of her status as a secondary consort. It is likely that at some point she did not see much hope for her son and made the heartbreaking decision to withdraw her support, perhaps hoping to protect her grandson from the rage of both king and prince. When ordering Seja's death, Yŏngjo claimed that it was a "secret" revealed to him by the prince's mother that had convinced him to force his suicide, but the record is obscure regarding the exact nature of the "secret" Lady Sŏn-hŭi revealed to the king.

In portraying the struggle between father and son, Oh probes their contrasting personalities: the king is quick and fiery; the prince, languid and shy. Although Yŏngjo wishes to project his image of a wise king, he is as morally flawed as his son. He may indeed be incensed by the prince's unrestrained sexuality, but at the same time this sixty-six-year-old king luxuriously indulges himself with a fifteen-year-old wife. Even though Seja suggests that his father is impotent, a psychoanalyst would not find it difficult to detect sexual rivalry between the two men. Yŏngjo's dilemma is that if he kills his son he will be without an heir. In this way, the confrontation of Yŏngjo and Seja is played out on at least three levels—king versus prince, father versus son, and man versus man.

In rendering this conflict into a modern play, Oh consulted several historical narratives. Among these the primary source was *A Journal Written in Silence* by Lady Hong, the prince's wife, which she managed to record many years after her husband's death (see JaHyun Kim Haboush's translation, listed in the Selected Bibliography). Much of the language in the play is taken directly from her account. Yŏngjo's outcry at the end, for example, "If I die, the three-hundred-year dynasty will end, but if you die, our dynasty will be preserved. So die then!" is a famous line that has reverberated in the hearts of Koreans since that time and up to the present day.

Oh sees the true subject of *Intimacy between Father and Son* as the "value of understanding" not only between father and son but, in a modern context, between all Koreans:

> *I believe that understanding is truly an important issue at a time when our country is divided in two. The struggle between Yŏngjo, who had to eliminate his own son for the sake of the dynasty, and the prince, who tries to survive, boils down to the issue of understanding and misunderstanding. As much as we need Molière, Shakespeare, and Mamet, we also need to deal with problems pertinent to us and to this peninsula. I read the history of the Chosŏn dynasty not as something that happened a long time ago, but as a story about real people. If we have a chance to look back and find faults in us now and in the Korean people in the context of history, then history is truly alive in us.*

Into his 1992 staging of *Intimacy between Father and Son*, Oh incorporated extensive visual and musical additions to the text, ranging from classical dance to contemporary popular songs. And in attempting to define Koreanness, he insisted that his actors adopt peculiarly Korean modes of behavior and expression. Oh has said that "Koreans traditionally do not look into each other's eyes when they speak; our communication is inherently indirect." Thus his characters often do not answer each other directly and, in staging his plays, he often asks actors, even in confrontational scenes, not to look at each other but to pretend to be preoccupied with something else (such as scratching the floor with a fingernail) or to face toward the audience throughout the scene. For similar reasons, Oh avoids what he calls "mid-height" in his plays—characters sitting on chairs around tables—because Koreans traditionally did not have such tables in their homes. Instead, his actors stand, sit, squat, and lie on the ground, free from the Western-style kitchen table that to Oh represents much of the aimlessness of modern Korean life.

Yet not all of the idiosyncrasies of Oh's practice as a stage director can be directly attributed to his interest in Korean culture.

Several images in *Intimacy between Father and Son* derive from Jerzy Grotowski's production of *The Constant Prince*, and much of his skill as a stage director lies in his ability constantly to surprise even his Korean audiences. He regularly thwarts the expectations of spectators by having his actors speak in unusual rhythms and breathe in idiosyncratic patterns. When we expect a character to react with horror or fear, for example—when forced to take poison, say—Oh may direct the actor to laugh like a child or perform an energetic dance. When we anticipate quick responses from the characters, Oh's actors often move with ritual gravity. Even when his dialogue is at its most realistic, one can never be sure that the performers will behave as we expect them to.

IN ATOMIZING KOREAN culture, Oh not only employs historical material but also relies heavily on traditional performance techniques and conventions. Although the story of *Ch'un-p'ung's Wife* (1976) is based on classic narratives, its dramatic vitality derives from the Korean theatrical traditions of *sandae nori* (a comprehensive term covering several forms of masked dance-drama, outdoor performance, ritual, and the like). In point of fact, *Ch'un-p'ung's Wife* may well be the most traditional play Oh has ever written, both in form and content, even if Western audiences might assume that its raucously absurdist tone lies far from what we might consider traditional.

The Korean classic *The Tale of Yi Ch'un-p'ung* provides the main story line of a married man who falls in love with a famous *kisaeng* (entertainment woman). When he runs out of money, the *kisaeng* kicks him out onto the street. The rest of the tale describes how the man's wife finds him and saves him from beggary. In the play, the wife is helped, not always effectively, by two amphibious characters, Yi Chi and Tŏk-jung, who derive from another Korean classic, *Song of the Underwater Palace*, an allegory satirizing human foibles by means of animal characters. The central figure in this story is a turtle named Pyŏljubu that crawls onto land in search of medicine for the ailing Sea King, just as Yi Chi and Tŏk-jung emerge from the sea in search of medicine for Yi Chi's eighty-year-old mother.

These materials have been cast into a form that veers away from their narrative roots and, instead, adheres more closely to the performance traditions of the *t'al ch'um,* the Korean masked dance-dramas that for centuries were performed in several of Korea's provinces. (See Cho Oh-kon's translation of five masked dance-dramas also listed in the Selected Bibliography.) As traditional Korea did not have indoor theater structures, performances were given at locations such as the foot of a hillside or a marketplace, where the performers could draw large audiences after seasonal and religious rites. Starting after dark under torchlight and continuing until dawn, performances of masked dance-theater began and ended with ritualistic ceremonies that surrounded dramatic episodes. Because its development was based on oral transmission, the masked dance-theater did not have written texts, and performances relied heavily on improvisation.

At its roots, Korean masked dance-drama is a form of satirical comedy. Performed for centuries by wandering professional actors for the common people, the dramas tend to turn normal social rules upside-down and openly discuss issues suppressed by the authorities: servant ridicules master, laymen mock priests, and wives argue with their husbands. To peasants living under a rigid feudal system, masked dance-theater provided a form of release from the pent-up resentments of generations of oppression. It is not surprising, therefore, that several contemporary Korean theater artists, including Oh T'ae-sŏk, have used the masked dance-drama to focus attention on current political and social tensions. *Ch'un-p'ung's Wife,* for instance, bears a strong resemblance to the seventh and last episode of the venerable *Pongsan* masked dance-drama. In the *Pongsan* drama, an old couple, who have been separated for a long time, finally reunite. But when the old woman learns that her husband has taken a concubine, she becomes so overwrought that she dies. The episode ends with a shaman's ritual to appease the dead woman's spirit by singing a prayer. In *Ch'un-p'ung's Wife*, similar rituals are offered, but with ludicrous results, as Oh wryly philosophizes on the absurdity of life and death.

Even in the early versions of the story, the character of the Wife is unconventional: she may be the first liberated woman in Korean literature, as she brazenly commits several of the "seven grounds for divorce," any one of which was traditionally considered a legitimate reason for sending a wife back to her parents' home. Contrary to this Confucian code, the Wife is jealous of her husband's concubine and freely speaks her mind. (In the play, the young Hwa-jo is also at fault for failing to pay proper respect to her husband's parents. Other grounds for divorce include infertility, lasciviousness, stealing, and serious illness.) At one point in the script, the Wife mentions a letter she sent to Ch'un-p'ung describing her death from "pent-up anger disease"—a recently recognized sickness disturbingly common among Korean women, who become physically ill as a result of living in a culture that prohibits them from displaying anger. The irony inheres not only in the fact that the letter is a lie, but that the outspoken Wife is one of the few older Korean women who would never die of such a disease.

By imbedding traditional performance practices within his modern plays (for instance, by having a male actor play the *kisaeng*), Oh exploits a complex cultural dialectic, because a century of Japanese and then American cultural hegemony had all but driven native Korean performance modes to extinction. Although the masked dance-dramas have since the 1970s been rediscovered by university students, most ancient theatrical forms remain unfamiliar to many Koreans or are viewed not as part of an ongoing tradition but as a revolutionary art form. Viewed metaculturally, then, the introduction of native theatrical traditions is both a memento of a nation's forgotten past and a new theatrical style as jarring to many Korean audiences as the Artaudian imagery that Oh juxtaposes with it. Ancient and avant-garde theatrical forms interrogate a postcolonial present, just as Oh's metacultural theater probes and mirrors the schizophrenic confusion of modern

Korean society, bombarded by the competing voices of East and West, old and new.

OH T'AE-SŎK ADDRESSES the problems of modern Korean society most directly in *Why Did Shim Ch'ŏng Plunge into the Sea Twice?* but still makes moving use of the dissonance between traditional Korean and Western narrative modes. The play was first presented at the fifteenth Seoul Theater Festival in 1991 and created immediate controversy by its brutal assault on Korea's indifference to such social problems as prostitution, crime, and violence—caused, Oh suggests, by rampant materialism.

Early in 1991, Oh read about a young man who had stabbed and killed a woman who was waiting to use a public phone booth. The woman, who was carrying her baby on her back, had asked the man to cut his telephone conversation short because she and several other people were waiting in line to use the same booth. Outraged and despondent over this brutal crime, Oh T'ae-sŏk wrote *Why Did Shim Ch'ŏng Plunge into the Sea Twice?* to raise a fundamental question addressed to his fellow Koreans. That question might be, to cite Ionesco, "Quelle est la morale?" or, more precisely, "Où est la morale?" In order to explore these questions, Oh transports a famous character from the past and makes her live once again in modern Korean society. In doing so, he both valorizes and deconstructs the ideals of the past.

The Song of Shim Ch'ŏng is a classic prose narrative as well as one of most popular of the five major works of traditional *p'ansori*, the art of oral storytelling in which a performer, accompanied by a drummer, sings and speaks an extended dramatized story. (Marshall Pihl's *The Korean Singer of Tales* is an excellent account of *p'ansori*, along with a complete translation of *The Song of Shim Ch'ŏng*.) In the *p'ansori* version, Shim Ch'ŏng is a virtuous girl born to a blind father. (Her mother died several days after giving birth to Shim Ch'ŏng.) As she grows up, her filial piety becomes known far and wide. One day a sly monk tells Shim Ch'ŏng's father that it is possible to cure his blindness if he will consecrate three hundred sacks of rice to a near-

by Buddhist temple. On hearing this news, her father is elated, but
soon despairs, for he realizes that to obtain such a large quantity of
rice is far beyond his means. Unable to accept her father's agony,
Shim Ch'ŏng sells herself to fishermen who are looking for a
young girl to sacrifice in order to appease the Sea King so that they
will have smooth sailing. Shim Ch'ŏng plunges into the waters of
Indangsu, naively believing that her father's blindness will be cured
as a result. While her father remains blind on earth, Shim Ch'ŏng
travels to a water palace, where she encounters her mother and is
eventually sent back to the world in a large lotus flower. The enor-
mous flower in which Shim Ch'ŏng travels back to the earth is
caught by fishermen and presented to the king. As the story goes,
the king discovers Shim Ch'ŏng in the flower and marries her. The
climax occurs when Shim Ch'ŏng, in search of her father, gives a
party for all of the blind men in the country; she finally sees her
father, wretched and still blind. Learning who Shim Ch'ŏng is, he
cries out, "Let me see your face!" whereupon he miraculously
regains his eyesight. The Confucian theme of the original story was
intended to promote filial piety, a philosophy widely accepted by
traditional Korean society. At the end, through her sacrifice, Shim
Ch'ŏng is transformed from a poor blind man's daughter to a
queen.

As usual, Oh T'ae-sŏk presents us with a wildly contemporary
version that discards the linear plot line of the traditional story.
Why Did Shim Ch'ŏng Plunge into the Sea Twice? begins the moment after
Shim Ch'ŏng has jumped into the sea and arrived at the water
palace of the Dragon King. Oh transforms the water palace into a
modern submarine fully equipped with the latest technology—
computers, machinery, and the like. In fact, the setting of the
Dragon King's submarine has reminded Korean critics of the control room in the Starship Enterprise of *Star Trek*.

The characters are also transformed to suit this futuristic back-
ground. The original Shim Ch'ŏng had always been portrayed as
beautiful, loyal, and completely devoted to her father. She
expressed not the slightest qualm about sacrificing herself to cure

her father's blindness. In contrast, Oh's Shim Ch'ŏng is far from obedient, sometimes stubborn, and even occasionally less than wholesome. In the introductory scene, for instance, she defies the Dragon King by insisting on accompanying him on a tour of the human world. The Dragon King, too, is a far cry from the solemn majesty of his prototype. Rather than the mysterious and omnipotent ruler of a great underwater kingdom, the Dragon King now behaves like a very ordinary human being—he is prurient, increasingly disreputable, and often ludicrous. To emphasize these changes, Oh avoids the stylized narrative of the classical versions and adopts brutally informal, everyday Korean language, although retaining, as he does in nearly all of his plays, a "three-four" rhythmic pattern (three syllables followed by four syllables), which he believes is the natural Korean cadence.

Because the Dragon King is unfamiliar with modern life, he needs a guide experienced in the ways of the city. His computer locates a young man, Chŏng Se-myŏng, once a struggling farmer but now reduced to selling frying pans in a sleazy market of the big city. In his descent from a hardworking farmer who dreamed of owning his own cattle farm to a hawker of shoddy wares in a ruthlessly materialistic society, Se-myŏng epitomizes the innocence and morality that Oh T'ae-sŏk believes many modern Koreans have lost. But the future holds even worse trials for Se-myŏng. Promising to make him rich, a stranger lures him into manufacturing and selling firebombs to demonstrators. This business takes place in a plastic hothouse, which provides a convenient symbol for Se-myŏng's fate. Plastic hothouses were originally built to grow vegetables in winter, but it is not uncommon for homeless people or illegal activities to reside in them. Made of vinyl, they are highly combustible. Hence the hothouses, like Se-myŏng, have descended from growing food and fostering life to hiding crime and abetting murder in a society ready to explode. The Dragon King carelessly tells Shim Ch'ŏng to set a small fire in the hothouse in order to scare Se-myŏng away from such shady dealings, but Se-myŏng's face is horribly deformed in a disastrous explosion. The

Dragon King is arrested for inciting arson and is thrown into jail, where he unexpectedly enjoys himself in learning details of the criminal underworld from fellow prisoners.

Wearing a white mask to cover his wounds, Se-myŏng finds work in an amusement park as a human target for a ball-tossing game. Months pass by. In the way of a capitalist success story, the degrading living-target game flourishes to the extent that the word "ORIGINAL" is added to a sign to distinguish it from other shooting galleries that apparently have mushroomed in imitation of Se-myŏng's. But Se-myŏng still dreams of running his own cattle farm, and the Dragon King, now well versed in the seamy side of life, tricks him into becoming a partner in a prostitution ring, which will be conducted from a boat supplying prostitutes to lonely bachelors who live on remote islands. When he learns the true purpose of their business venture, Se-myŏng tries to send the women back to their homes by a scheme to pay off their considerable debts. He demands that a television auction be held on board the ship in which each woman will be "saved" by the highest bidder. He suggests to the girls that if no one offers to take care of their debts, then the world has ultimately betrayed them and they may as well jump into the sea. One after another, the faces of girls appear on the television screen, but no one bids for them. Volunteering to substitute herself for a girl who is afraid to die, Shim Ch'ŏng once again plunges into the sea—but this time without hope of resurrection.

Recent productions of *Shim Ch'ŏng* have raised painful issues for its Korean audiences, chief among them, perhaps, the question that Bertolt Brecht asked in *Der gute Mensch von Sezuan*: Why can't a virtuous person live in modern society? Under Oh T'ae-sŏk's freewheeling direction, the script translated here serves as only a basic framework for his production. He inserts scenes featuring bodily movements, sound, and music (classical and modern Korean popular songs, in addition to Western rock music), and fills the stage with cardboard boxes and dozens of puppets based on traditional Korean models. In a vignette that takes place before the beginning of the play, actors scattered throughout the theater shout loudly trying to attract customers, who are in fact the audience members entering the theater. Standing in the midst of piles of cardboard boxes, the actors look like street hawkers advertising cheap trinkets. According to the theater critic Kim Yun-cheol, "It was not difficult to grasp that the warehouse was a microcosm of Korean society, possibly the global village, which has grown bleak due to materialism, dehumanization, and the loss of identity."

ALTHOUGH HIS INTEREST in native Korean performance traditions is profound, Oh T'ae-sŏk's search for a Korean theater is neither a reaction against Western influence nor a museum for Korean nostalgia. His plays and stage directing show a clear respect for Artaud's theater of cruelty and the social *Gestussen* of Brecht's epic theater even as they explore native themes. But whereas some Korean theater artists ignore Korea's theatrical heritage and others attempt to preserve it in a pure form or to bring it up to date, Oh breaks down traditions and reconstructs them in a new theatrical form that challenges both old and current conventions alike. Most of his actors at the Mokhwa Repertory Company are well trained in traditional music and dance but at the same time follow a spiritual regimen equivalent in intensity to that demanded by Grotowski. And just as Grotowski's theater pieces evoked a sense of sacredness in Poland, so Oh's plays strike Koreans as the rebirth of rituals they no longer knew they remembered.

Audiences must judge for themselves whether Oh's admixture of East and West, old and new, yields a seamless unity or a fractured aggregation of parts. What seems to matter to Oh is that cultures be explored as cultures and in relation to other cultures. His search for Koreanness, then, is not a sentimental rummaging through tried-and-true ideals, but rather a concerted program of comparison and change. In a 1992 interview, Oh T'ae-sŏk explained this concept of mutable Korean tradition as follows:

> *Our theatrical traditions never had any fixed forms, as do Japan's noh and kabuki theaters. In Japan a performer enters the structure of a form at an*

early age and then moves on to develop his own artistry in it. Well, then, why don't we have such forms? Wouldn't it have been nice if we had a similarly formalized tradition? But listen to Korean music and its changdan *[rhythmic patterns]. It never keeps the same beat. Our tradition has always avoided set forms. It has descended to us not in a fixed state, but in an ever-flowing fashion. Our tradition has grown spontaneously. It constantly changes, reflecting current situations because it is innately fluid.*

Given this view of Korean tradition and his reluctance to follow fixed theatrical conventions, Oh may indeed have found genuine Koreanness. In the most radical sense, his metacultural theater views cultures as processes that may be modified in the theater, but only by being considered as processes in relation to other processes. His refusal to adhere to fixed forms, even his own, lies at the core of the energy that makes Oh T'ae-sŏk's experiments so probing and unexpected.

TRANSLATORS' NOTE

ALTHOUGH THESE TRANSLATIONS are intended for a general, English-speaking public (whether performers, spectators, or readers), we have retained a modified version of the standard McCune-Reischauer romanization of Korean words so that actors, should they undertake to pronounce them more or less accurately, will have a reliable guide. Unfortunately, any complete system of romanizing Korean requires the use of diacritical marks, which seem to intimidate all but the most sympathetic reader.

Non-Korean speakers will not go too far astray, however, if they remember that an apostrophe (') following a consonant indicates a strong aspiration of the consonant, and that a breve (˘) above a vowel indicates that the sound is produced farther down and back in the mouth, close to English *u* [ʌ] as in *cup*. Double unvoiced consonants are pronounced close to their voiced counterparts, with a tension in the throat and mouth. Although there are long and short vowels, Korean syllables take very even stress. Note that *ae* and *oe* in McCune-Reischauer represent single sounds, while other combinations of vowels generally do not. Elsewhere, romanized Korean words should be pronounced as they would be in English; such, at any rate, was the intention of McCune and Reischauer in creating their system. A brief pronunciation guide to Korean vowels is offered below, but the advice of a native speaker is clearly desirable.

Although attempts to approximate Korean pronunciation may well foster an evocative Korean mood, English-speaking actors

should perhaps not attempt to duplicate Korean sounds unless
they are thoroughly comfortable doing so. If performers cannot
say such words easily and naturally, then the audience's experience
may more closely resemble that of overhearing a language lesson
than listening to a play. Actors, of course, are always free to make
such modifications as seem necessary.

    We follow McCune-Reischauer throughout the play texts, but
not in the case of the playwright's family name, which he spells
"Oh." Personal names are given in their Korean order: family name
followed by given name. In addition to proper nouns, a few other
Korean words remain untranslated in these English versions, the
most frequent being the mournful cry of pain or relief after endur-
ing pain, *aigoo*, frequently heard at funerals, after physical injury, or
at less serious moments of anguish.

McCUNE-REISCHAUER	INTERNATIONAL PHONETIC ALPHABET	EQUIVALENTS
i	[i] or [ɪ]	create, ink
o	[ou] or [o]	home, solo
ŏ	[ʌ]	but
e	[ɛ]	met
a	[ɑ]	father
u	[u]	do
ŭ	[ʌ] or [ə]	but, taken
ae	[æ]	hat
oe	[ø]	Köln

BICYCLE

Cast of Characters

YUN CHIN, *a clerk of the town registry office*
KU, *another clerk of the town registry office*
IM, *a schoolteacher*
HAN, *a villager, father of the House of Geese*
YOUNG WOMAN, *thought to be the eldest daughter of the House of Geese*
CHILD, *thought to be the second daughter of the House of Geese*
Man from SOLMAE, *a leper*
His WIFE, *also a leper*
An herbal DOCTOR, *now deceased*
OLD MAN
HWANG SŎK-KU, *a crippled liquor distiller*
Two GRAVE DIGGERS
YOUNG MAN, *a mourner*
OWNER *of Persimmon-Tree House*
His SERVANT
VOICE *of a north Korean soldier*
YUN CHIN'S UNCLE *from Yesan, a survivor of the registry fire*
SO KWAN-HO, *the other survivor of the registry fire*

TOWN REGISTRY OFFICE

YUN: How about writing an absence report for me?
KU: What do you want me to say?

YUN: Well, listen, here's a rough draft. *(Reading from a note in his hand.)* "One night I fainted because the ghost of a young woman called out to me from her grave by the side of the road. I was so scared that I began to shake and, later, I got sick. Because of this, I missed forty-two days of work. Whereupon I submit this report of absence."

KU: You're going to send that in?

YUN: Well, I guess I have to, unless I make up some outright lies, because that's what happened. This is why I really need your help.

KU: But what happened? You've got to tell me the whole thing.

YUN: *(Pause.)* I was having a rough day. I'd turned in my high school friend to the police for practicing medicine without a license. He was just a quack. All he knew about medicine was what he had learned in the army as a nurse. I couldn't let him keep doing that. So, I sent a report about him to the police station. I was about to have a cigarette when I found this girl about fourteen or fifteen standing right in front of me holding a medical report issued by the Provincial Hospital. Said she came to register the death of her sister. But the family registry worker had already left for the day. I asked where she came from. "Munjang Village," she said. She'd come a long way, so I handled her case and did the paperwork. Her sister had died of tuberculosis at age nineteen, worst luck . . .

KU: Was that the girl? The ghost you ran into? You said somebody called to you.

YUN: *(Shaking his head.)* I'm not sure if I heard a voice. I was totally discombobulated. I couldn't hear anything. It was like I was drowning in water.

KU: Wait a second. You're skipping part of the story. I don't follow you. So what happened after you took care of the death certificate at the office?

YUN: I had a couple of drinks at Naesan's. I was feeling real out of sorts. For the first time in my life I had turned in someone knowing that it would hurt a lot of people. So, I had a few drinks. Later, the Naesan woman told me to leave my bicycle behind, since it would be difficult to drag along. But I felt sort of empty without it, so I decided to push it beside me as I walked. I thought I walked pretty far, but in fact I'd barely climbed over Nŏkpae Hill. *(He starts walking, dragging along his bicycle which has been parked beside him.* KU *follows.)*

NŎKPAE HILL

*(*IM, *an elementary school teacher, approaches from one side, dragging his bicycle. He is holding a flashlight.* KU *steps to the other side.* YUN *and* IM *park their bicycles in one corner of the stage.)*

IM: On your way home now? It's real late.

YUN: How about you? You on night duty?

IM: Oh, no, the family's holding the memorial service at the big house, you know. I guess you'll be having a memorial service tonight, too, eh?

YUN: Is tonight the eighth? I almost forgot.

IM: *(Lighting a cigarette, squats down.)* They delivered the memorial stone to the town registry building. Said it came from Hong-sŏng. Anyhow, it's a black stone.

YUN: Black, you say? Must be obsidian, after all the talk about marble.

IM: It's good, hard stone. Besides, black's right for a memorial.

YUN: They're supposed to have it up before the end of the year, I hear.

IM: It took them three years just to decide on the stone. *(Holding the cigarette in his mouth, starts off with his bike.)* We might have frost tonight, what with all this fog. Down below there's a hut near the stone bridge. You'll see a light there, but watch your step in the dark.

YUN: I see. Good-bye. You take care of yourself, too.

*(*IM *exits.)*

KU: *(Coming forward.)* What are they building at the registry?

YUN: The memorial, you see. Don't you know about it? During the occupation, the town registry—that's where the town registry building used to be before the war. They say a hundred twenty-seven people, most of them pretty well known in this town, were locked up inside it, accused of being anticommunists. The nationalist army was pushing up from the south. The bastards from the north were in the middle of retreating, so they set fire to the building with everyone inside. Tonight, at least a hundred families are holding memorial services for the dead. No, not tonight—I mean, "that night." Look, if I keep telling the story this way, it'll only confuse you. Why don't we do it like this? I'll do exactly what I did that night, so you won't have to try to figure out what it was like. Just imagine it's happening tonight.

KU: All right. We'll pretend it's all happening tonight. Then what?

YUN: I thought about taking a nap in a seedbed of rice. But I couldn't because I remembered that my uncle from Yesan would be making a scene at my house, cutting his face with a piece of glass and . . . (*Shaking his head.*) He was there at the registry building, you see, the night of the fire. Just two men survived, and he happened to be one of them. Let's see, my father's his older brother. My uncle says it's shameful he came out alive—that he didn't save his brother. On each anniversary night, he takes over the living room and cuts his face with a piece of glass. (*With his finger, he mimes cutting across his forehead.*) He gouges in, line by line, like the furrows of a rice field . . . the blood dripping down his face. (*Shakes his head and pushes his bicycle along.*) If we go down a little more, it's only three miles to Shintŭlmae Gully. There's a couple of houses there. The house of lepers is farther on in Solmae, and right before an intersection that leads up a hill called Saengbae is another house. The family there's called the House of Geese because they raise geese. His name's Han, though—he's a good man, a living Buddha, to tell the truth, but his wife's got a bad case of epilepsy. He and his wife haven't lived near a soul for some twenty years now. Once he wanted to plant some things in a small lot out behind his house, so I helped him get a permit to work it. Somehow or other Han thinks I gave him the land. Every day he comes out to say hello. Look at him. Even this late at night, he's waiting for me.

The House of Geese

(HAN *has been looking out over a fence made of trifoliate orange trees. Seeing* YUN *approaching,* HAN *walks around the fence to greet him.* HAN *holds a small box which he ties to the rear seat of* YUN*'s bicycle.* KU *steps aside.*)

YUN: Now, what are you are tying on there?

HAN: I gathered some *tŏdŏk* roots for you. But I don't think they're big enough to put on the memorial altar.

YUN: But I could be fired for taking a bribe, you know.

HAN: (*Taking out a small folded note from his sleeve.*) Just a while ago, back home, my kids read this note for me. I couldn't imagine the little one would do such a thing. (*Lights a match so that* YUN *can read the note.*)

CHILD'S VOICE: (*As* YUN *reads the note.*) Weather, clear. I helped my sister Chi-yŏng with her homework in handicrafts by cutting up two potatoes. I hear the sound of a train coming from town. Is that train going up north or going down south? Which train should I take? I don't know.

HAN: That's my number two. She's only fourteen.

YUN: She ran away? When?

HAN: After lunch, nobody saw her. If she took the train like she says here, she must've gone to the city. But I never thought she could do such a thing.

YUN: Does she know anyone in the city?

HAN: Nobody. Who would she know? She's never been outside this town, not even to the market.

YUN: But who gave you this note? What did your oldest one say?

HAN: All she can do is choke back tears.

YUN: Let me talk to her for a second.

HAN: (*Calling over the fence.*) Hey! Are you there? (*Goes around the fence into the house.*)

YUN: *(To* KU.*)* You've got to promise me something now. Don't tell anyone what you're going to hear—what the oldest one and I talked about. Just listen and think about it.

*(*KU *nods. Suddenly, there is the sound of honking as* HAN, *chasing geese in one direction, goes away into the backyard of the house. The sound of two people talking is heard. A* YOUNG WOMAN, *about twenty years old, comes out. One notices her peculiar demeanor even before her shabby clothes. She neither bows nor looks at* YUN. *As a consequence, she may appear to be a person of low intelligence who is stubborn and insensitive. She speaks as if she were talking to herself, unaware of* YUN*'s presence.)*

YOUNG WOMAN: *(Pause.)* I sent my sister away.

YUN: What do you mean, "sent her away"?

YOUNG WOMAN: Last year they brought us a newborn baby from the house across the way.

YUN: From the house of lepers?

YOUNG WOMAN: My sister would have been shocked to find out that we adopted the baby. One day last month, she asked me if she came from the same family.

YUN: Did anyone else come from that house?

YOUNG WOMAN: *(Pause. Nods.)* A boy. He started grammar school this year. My sister didn't know anything about us taking him in because she was too young then even to know what adoption was.

YUN: So what happened? Did she figure out she came from the same house?

YOUNG WOMAN: Their house is a lot farther away than it looks. But whenever she saw anything in front of it, she started shaking— like my mom does in one of her fits. At night, when I'm sleeping, she comes over and examines my face, feels it with her hand, over and over, and then checks her own face. Then she stares into my eyes, and that scared me to death. *(She shudders.)* I drove her out because I was scared. Anyway, she couldn't live that way. Neither could I.

YUN: But where could she have gone? How could you drive her away like that? Do you mean to the lepers' house?

YOUNG WOMAN: *(Startled, crouches down, embracing herself by grabbing her elbows. She gags several times as if something were caught in her throat.)* I wonder if she did go to the house over there. Once I saw her grab a goose by the neck and twist it. She said that in a dream her mom came to see her and that a goose bit off her mom's finger. Now she was twisting the goose for the finger, because she wanted to give it back to her mom.

YUN: Did she come from the lepers' house, then?

YOUNG WOMAN: She came along when I was six. I don't know. *(Suddenly stares at him.)* Did she come from there, too?

YUN: I asked you that question.

YOUNG WOMAN: In my dream, I . . . I . . . I set fire to that house. In a dream . . .

YUN: Are you all right? Is she all right now?

YOUNG WOMAN: I can't even hang the wash up on the line. When I see clothes swaying in the wind, I feel sick because they look like the people from that house. While making a fire, if I hear wood cracking, I count the fingers on my hand, because I think a finger broke off and is burning like a stick of kindling. If *I'm* like this, can you imagine what was going through that little girl's mind? Poor thing. I didn't drive her away to die. I didn't. I wanted her to live. I wanted her to go far away and forget Mom and me and . . . live!

YUN: But you're old enough to know what the world's like. How could you chase her out of the house like that? Did you reckon she could beg meals out there? She can't beg for food, you know.

YOUNG WOMAN: But that's her fate.

YUN: I can't believe what she's saying. Do you think your father gets anything for raising you children?

YOUNG WOMAN: *(Quivers in anger.)* The girl who ran away didn't think so. She washed the little ones and rocked them to sleep. She loved them very much. She was simply scared. She ran away out of fear. Fear.

(She turns away to go inside the house. The sound of geese erupts several times and then subsides. A sense of gloom falls over the stage.)

YUN: *(To* KU.*)* I'd gotten into it this far, so I decided to walk toward
the house at Solmae.

KU: To the lepers' house—so late at night? To do what?

YUN: Well, what else could I do? I had this sinking feeling in my
chest, thinking about the little girl, nowhere to be found, far
away from home. *(Walks his bicycle. A bell attached to the wheels rings
a couple of times. As if in response to this, geese honk wildly, but then their
sounds rapidly subside.)* You see? These days, the most common
thing in the world around here is a runaway kid. And once a kid
runs away, she's gone, and that's it. At least you can do something about a quack who cuts open people's guts without knowing the first thing about medicine. All you have to do is turn
him in. But with a runaway child, it's different. What drove her
away from home?—I just had to find out, don't you see? And
whose kid is she anyway?—That's what I had to find out first. So
I started walking toward Solmae. And I saw the man from
Solmae coming from the opposite direction. Like he was waiting
for me.

*(Out of the darkness, the man from the Solmae house of lepers emerges. He is
wearing a worn-out plastic bag over his clothes tied around his waist with a
string, like fishermen are normally dressed. A towel is wrapped around his face
and a straw hat sits on top of his head, over the towel. He offers* YUN *two boxes
of candles by politely extending both hands, on which he wears long, red plastic gloves.)*

SOLMAE: I heard you were holding a memorial service tonight.

YUN: *(Takes the candle boxes and tucks them under straps on the rear carrying-
rack of his bicycle.)* How are you doing these days?

SOLMAE: Well, it looks like we'll be doing so-so this year. Peppers
may be okay, but the cabbages don't look good at all. Maybe the
seeds were bad; the cabbage leaves are all turning kind of yellow.
Seems like they won't do as good as other people's, anyway.
Now, watch your step as you go.

*(As he disappears into darkness, the rustling noise of his plastic clothes trails
behind him.)*

KU: You know, you seem to get more respect around here than a cabinet minister. I don't think most people would bring out a box of candles on a night like this, even if a damned cabinet minister walked by.

YUN: It's only because the man is lonely.

KU: But, by the way, you forgot to ask him whose child the girl was.

YUN: I couldn't, what with him popping out like that all of a sudden. Anyway, I felt somehow it wasn't the right moment.

KU: Yeah, you're right. Besides, it's really the House of Geese's problem. *(Starts rolling the bicycle beside him. The bell on the bicycle wheel rings.)*

YUN: Over there, sitting in the outhouse by the three-way intersection, is the herbal doctor who passed away at the time of the registry fire.

KU: What?

YUN: At first I thought some guy from another town had taken one drop too many. *(He parks his bicycle and sits on its seat.)*

THREE-WAY INTERSECTION

(A small, temporary outhouse for farmers is seen. Without a roof, it consists entirely of three walls of sedge mat only waist-high. An apparition of a DOCTOR, once a practitioner of Chinese herbal medicine, is seated inside the outhouse with only his face showing. He wears a traditional outer coat, as he did while alive. As the heavy fog gathers, he appears at first glance to be bathing in a muddy lake, with his head just above water.)

DOCTOR: Got a light?

(YUN gets off his bicycle, his head darting in all directions. He listens. YUN's movements are slightly confused in this scene; the confusion is particularly evident in how he gauges distance and direction.)

DOCTOR: Got a light?

YUN: Yes.

DOCTOR: It's me. Me.

YUN: But . . . who are you?

DOCTOR: Give me a light.

YUN: Yeah . . . I'm just looking for a match here.

(*He strikes a match, but his shaking hands cause the matches remaining in the match box to rattle. The burning match illuminates the* DOCTOR's *face, which does not yet have a cigarette in its mouth. The* DOCTOR *blows the light out.* YUN *lights another match. The* DOCTOR *blows it out again.* YUN *lights yet another match.*)

YUN: Ouch! It's hot! Are you drunk or something? (*Rubs the inside of his hand.*)

KU: What do you keep striking matches for? You've been drinking too much lately. If you keep tossing it down like that, you'll have a hell of a time when you're old, you know.

YUN: (*To the* DOCTOR.) Did you get the light?

DOCTOR: Are you the grandson of Se-hwan from Hangaengee?

YUN: Yes, I am. But who are you?

DOCTOR: Riding on a bike like that, you look exactly like your grandfather. Just like him.

YUN: How did you know my grandfather?

DOCTOR: I left your dad just now. Your dad must be home by now. You should hurry, it's late.

YUN: Where did you two go?

DOCTOR: We went to the market to get some arrowroots. We couldn't find anything good, though. There was only a handful of them and they were only the size of my finger. Much too small. Why are you standing there like that? Go home. Hurry up, now!

YUN: Okay, okay, I'm going. Take care.

DOCTOR: Go on. I'm done here, too.

(YUN *unlocks the bicycle and lifts it up to put on his shoulder as if he were crossing a stream. He falters backwards a few steps. The* DOCTOR *stands up, pulls up his trousers, and wraps a belt around his waist. The old man is quite meticulous in carefully unwrapping the straw string that had been holding the long outer clothes around his waist. Coming out of the outhouse, he tucks a broken straw broom [which he had put aside] in a cleft of the sedge mat of the outhouse and walks away leisurely.* YUN, *still holding his bicycle on his shoulder, watches as the old man disappears.* KU, *who has been hidden by fog, emerges. In this scene,* KU *has not been able to see the* DOCTOR. *He can only conjec-*

ture from YUN*'s strange behavior that* YUN *has encountered an apparition.*)

KU: So you stood there like that the whole time?

YUN: (*Parks his bicycle.*) You saw the old man, didn't you? He was having a grand old time here in the outhouse. (KU *shakes his head.*) Didn't you hear us talking?

KU: I did, but I only heard you say, "Who are you? . . . Yeah, I'm just looking for a match here . . . Did you get a light?" What did he say?

YUN: He's already gone.

KU: (*As if warming his hand over a fire, he stretches his hand to touch the broken broom tucked in the cleft of the outhouse.*) But what does your grandfather have to do with it? You were talking about him, too.

YUN: Yŏsubaemi Lake is on the way to the Saengbae fields, isn't it? My grandfather drowned in the lake on his way back from seeing his mistress in town. He was talking about it.

KU: Is the lake deep enough to drown in?

YUN: Oh, no. Even when the lake's high, the water only comes up to your chest. Even so, my grandfather died mysteriously with his head above water, sitting on his bike. He died sitting straight up, pretty as a picture.

KU: The bike was on top of the water?

YUN: (*Parks his bicycle.*) Well, they say the bike was standing just like this, right in the middle of Yŏsubaemi Lake.

KU: But who did it?

YUN: We don't know. Everybody felt it was some sort of foul play, but there was never any evidence. We always thought someone might have done something to him because, before independence, he'd been a policeman at the station. I pass by the lake all the time, but I've never seen him. Then this doctor was telling me that I look exactly like my grandfather.

KU: Look here, do you see these ghosts a lot?

YUN: The souls are busy tonight.

KU: You know, you need to find yourself a goat, a whole goat, cook it real good, and eat it like medicine. And if I were you, I wouldn't eat just one, but a whole lot of them.

YUN: Didn't you hear me screaming "It's hot!" after lighting one of the matches? I thought the head of a match had stuck to the palm of my hand. But it didn't. Later I found a scratch from somebody's fingernail. *(Opening his palm.)* Here. Ah, it's healed now. This is the scratch.

KU: It works, you know. Goat's the only cure for this.

YUN: I saw a lot of blood on my palm.

KU: It's not good to see ghosts so much. Have a goat or two before things get out of hand. I know a guy who was guarding a melon patch at night who saw some ghosts. He raced out of the shed to catch them. They found him later—drowned in the reservoir. In fact, it was Brother Il-yŏl who died that way.

YUN: Is that right? He died like that, huh?

(They both walk their bicycles, and the bells on the wheels ring.
In the distance, an OLD MAN *is seen crouching down, hanging a small lantern in a crab-fishing hut.)*

KU: Well now, somebody's taking some time off. Free time like that's hard to come by these days.

YUN: That man closed his cloth shop last year after he got robbed walking back from P'angyo Market. He sits there hoping to catch the robber. The district manager says he'll catch him someday.

CRAB-FISHING HUT AT THE STONE BRIDGE

(A humpbacked stone bridge only ten feet long and four feet wide; although quite small, it is made of a single, huge stone. It is old and magnificent, as though someone long ago had sculpted a turtle-shaped memorial stone and placed it across the river. Under one end of the bridge is a crab-fishing hut made of straw, shaped like a kitchen drainer turned upside-down. An OLD MAN *arranges a lantern in the hut so that its light lures crabs into a net as they crawl up toward the rice fields. The* OLD MAN *is a rural villager who has managed to purchase a rice field by peddling cloth in the city. Used to a life of wandering, he habitually leaves home to visit the hut.* YUN *parks his bicycle and*

approaches the hut, while KU *sits on the stone bridge.)*

YUN: You've caught quite a few crabs this evening.

OLD MAN: Who are you?—Hush, listen to that! Did you hear it?

YUN: What?

OLD MAN: *(Listens.)* They must be butchering something down in the valley—on the sly. They were making noises like that the other night, and they're doing it again tonight.

YUN: Butchering down in the valley?

OLD MAN: Sure, they do it there because it's near the river spring but far away from people passing by.

(The two men listen for a moment. YUN *catches a crab, takes it from the net, and puts it in a bucket.)*

YUN: Ah, this one keeps running away from me.

OLD MAN: It mustn't be.

YUN: I hear someone coming.

(A crippled liquor distiller, HWANG SŎK-KU, *emerges from the darkness. Infuriated about something, he is breathing hard and also drags a bicycle. On the rear of his bike are two white plastic liquor barrels hanging on either side of the rear wheel.)*

HWANG: No one's going to believe this. Who could believe that I, Hwang Sŏk-ku, just took a dive into the manure pile because a cow kicked me in the butt? Not one soul in this town would believe such a story except me, Hwang Sŏk-ku. Damn it!

OLD MAN: What's that smell? Why the hell did you come around here smelling like that? Get out of here!

HWANG: Well, thanks a lot! If I go to the shop like this, it'll stink up the liquor.

OLD MAN: So, instead, you decide to splash shit around here when I'm trying to catch crabs?

HWANG: You know the Persimmon-Tree House over at Sŏndong Village? With an outhouse right beside the cow shed? I was in the outhouse minding my own business. The plank under my left foot creaked—it wasn't put in right. So I bent over to fix it, and, god almighty, this thing called a cow must have thought my butt was a barn or something. It bumped me hard right in the ass. I could easily be dead by now with my nose stuck in a pile of shit. I was so pissed off, I decided to show it who was boss—me, Hwang Sŏk-ku. So I says to the cow, "Now, you're dead!" And I grabbed that cow by the horns and kicked it hard, right in the stomach. It started jumping around, all over the place, till it leaps out of the shed, smashing up everything. So I shout, "The cow's jumping! The cow's jumping!" And the whole family runs out of the house and chases after it.

YUN: Good heavens! What a mess for them!

HWANG: Who gives a damn about somebody else's troubles around here? There was a big fuss tonight at your house, too, you know.

YUN: Was our cow jumping around, too?

HWANG: The old man's face . . . oh, god . . . it looked like a snake shedding its skin. The blood poured down his face . . . over his eyes and nose. His whole face was red, covered with blood. I can't describe it.

(YUN *climbs up the stone bridge where* KU *is standing;* HWANG *and the* OLD MAN *freeze.*)

YUN: *(To* KU.*)* Here now, remember that part of the story—when the cow was running wild, 'cause I think I heard the sound of a cow jumping myself.

KU: A cow jumping at night?

YUN: Farther away, though, over in Shintŭlmae Gully.

KU: Then the guy's story isn't hogwash, is it?

YUN: Well, I don't know about that.

KU: But the Old Man said something about a cow, too, didn't he?

YUN: Eh?

KU: Didn't he say something about people making noise, butchering something? That there was some funny business going on across the gully?

YUN: All he saw was a couple of guys putting sod on a grave. A couple of days later, I found out they were secretly burying someone—the dead girl from Munjang Village. I ran into them later.

(YUN *steps down to the hut, and* HWANG *resumes speaking in his previous manner.*)

HWANG: And this guy was having a big fight with Tong-sŏn's mother. Tong-sŏn's family farmed a small field right over your father's grave, didn't they?

YUN: Yeah, I know this spring they worked some land—no bigger than the back of my hand.

HWANG: Tong-sŏn's family must have been fertilizing it. This guy was complaining that putting fertilizer on top of a grave was disrespectful to the dead. But who was that guy? Is he related to you?

YUN: He's my uncle from Yesan. Every year on the anniversary night of my father's death, he cuts his face with a piece of broken glass.

HWANG: Come to think of it, tonight's the memorial night for the old registry building.

OLD MAN: Hush . . . Listen to that.

HWANG: What is it?

OLD MAN: Don't you hear a noise from the gully?

HWANG: On the way over here I saw some people putting sod on a grave.

YUN: Sodding a grave—at night?

OLD MAN: I thought they were secretly killing something.

HWANG: I'm gonna catch those guys. Just you wait and see.

OLD MAN: But how can you with your legs?

HWANG: What do you mean with my legs? These legs did just fine when I was the first nationalist soldier to make it back to town after we pushed the North Koreans out. I rode into town with Korean flags stuck all over my bicycle.

YUN: You don't say! Flags flying on your bike, eh?

HWANG: You bet. The mayor of Kilsan had fixed up a bike with flags all over it to welcome us. I asked him if my brother was okay, and he gave the bike to me. Told me to go home. I was peddling it across Saengbae field. People had just begun harvesting the rice. I could see my house in the distance. *(He shouts an exclamation of tearful relief.)* Aigoo! I was crying like a baby. I yelled out at the top of my lungs, "I'm coming home! I'm coming home alive!" I saw townspeople running toward me, and I got off the bike. Then I felt this sharp pain in my leg. It was a bamboo knife, wider than my hand, sticking out of my leg like a cow's horn. Somehow this gigantic knife got stuck deep in my leg. *Aigoo!* I fainted when I saw it. *(He pulls up his pants to show the scar.)*

YUN: I never knew that before. I always thought you got hurt in the war. But who would do such a thing?

HWANG: The old man, Chi-hwan. He died soon after that.

OLD MAN: He'd been tortured for keeping the night school going during the occupation and went crazy.

HWANG: Damn it all! I was so sad when Chi-hwan passed away. *(Blows his nose.)* Well, what are you standing around here for? Get home fast. Your uncle was starting to calm down, but who knows what he's up to by now.

(YUN rolls along on his bicycle. The bell from the bicycle rings.)

SHINTŬLMAE GULLY

KU: Do you remember your father?

YUN: Not at all. I was barely a year old when he passed away.

KU: So you don't have any memories of him?

YUN: I'm just like my mom. I think of my uncle from Yesan as my father, just like she does.

KU: What did your father do for a living?

YUN: He was assistant principal at the school. Once he fell out of a persimmon tree at school and broke his foot. So every day he had to stick his foot in the damn urine bucket. My mom says his left shoulder got permanently bent out of shape—like this. She does a good imitation of him, but I can't.

(At this moment, two GRAVE DIGGERS emerge from the darkness at the other side of the stage. One is carrying a small coffin in his traditional backpack

[A-frame carrier], while the other's backpack is empty. A YOUNG MAN *wearing a mourner's hemp cap follows the* GRAVE DIGGERS. YUN *and* KU *step aside to allow them to pass by.)*

YUN: Where are you all going?

YOUNG MAN: To Oejang.

YUN: Where's Oejang?

YOUNG MAN: Past Kwiam.

YUN: That's a long way to go, did you know that?

YOUNG MAN: And we have to take the back roads.

YUN: It'll take you a lot longer that way. You'll have to hurry to get there before dawn.

(The GRAVE DIGGERS *quickly disappear.)*

YUN: From the looks of them, I think they're grave diggers.

KU: If they aren't, what's that coffin for?

YUN: To trick people like me. I turned the corner, see? Here we are. Now you take the bicycle—it'll make it easy to explain exactly what happened. *(KU takes over the bicycle.)* I came around the corner and thought I saw a fox in the distance. But it vanished just like that. A second later the girl from the House of Geese steps up behind my bicycle.

(A CHILD, *the second daughter of the House of Geese, sits on the rear rack of* YUN's *bicycle.* KU *acts as* YUN *in this scene, while* YUN *continues to explain the situation.)*

KU: Good heavens! What's this now? Where did you come from?

YUN: She scared me to death. I asked her where she'd been, and she told me she'd been hiding in the graveyard since sundown. Said she stayed there 'cause she knew people would be scared to look for her in a graveyard.

(The CHILD *freezes catatonically as if she were a stage prop. Not even a hair moves. Her face is frozen with fear. It is clear that* YUN *must have used a great deal of patience to coax her into speaking.)*

KU: So she didn't go to the train station after all?

YUN: She was scared.

KU: Well why didn't she go home?

YUN: She was scared.

KU: But what was she going to do?

YUN: Nothing. She was just trembling. She'd been in the graveyard
all by herself. Can you imagine what must it have been like?
When she heard the sound of my bike, she ran down to the road
thinking it might be her schoolteacher or the town clerk. She
just started running down here. But I worked on her, coaxed
her little by little. Finally I talked her into going back home.
Then I turned the bike in the other direction. Now, turn the
bike around.

(KU *turns the bike. The* CHILD *sits on the rear rack. A strange and subtle
change comes over her. She straightens from the waist up and leans forward,
staring ahead.*)

YUN: I lit candles on the bike to calm her down. Light two candles,
please.

(KU *stations the bicycle so he can take candles out of the box that the* SOL-
MAE *leper gave to* YUN. YUN *makes a fire with some paper taken from a plastic bag.* KU *attaches the two candles to the handlebars by tying them with
straw. The candles swing enchantingly. Completely lost in thought, the* CHILD
stares at the candle flames.)

YUN: I asked if she knew who I was, and I told her that I was the
town clerk, Yun. She nodded. I told her not to worry about her
dad because I'd tell him nice things about her. Then I was hoping to bring her out of it, so I told her the story of the bicycle
with the Korean flags. I said, "There was a big war a long time
ago. A soldier was coming home from battle after winning the
war. He rode across Saengbae field riding a bike with Korean
flags on each handlebar. They say he shouted, 'I'm coming
home! I'm coming home alive!' Well now, you're riding with
candles instead of flags. So why don't you yell like the soldier?
'I'm coming home! I'm coming back home!'"

(*At this moment the* CHILD *lets out a shriek, jumps down from the bicycle,
and starts pulling it backwards as if she were in a rope-pulling contest. She
screams with fear, and with her finger indicates that someone is coming from
the direction the bicycle faces.* KU *and the bicycle tumble down together,*

KU'S *body intertwined with the bicycle. The child quickly disappears into the* *darkness.)*

KU: Where's she going? Why's she doing that?

YUN: She grabbed my waist. Said someone's coming. I couldn't hear a thing, but she was sure somebody was coming—that we had to run away from whoever it was. I tried to calm her down, but she bit my hand and ran away. So I said, "Stop," and turned my bicycle around to find a man standing in my way.

(From the side opposite to the direction in which the CHILD *ran, there is the* *rustling of a plastic garment. The* SOLMAE *leper appears as before.)*

YUN: I felt sure something was wrong, so I stopped him and asked where he was going. *(To* KU.*)* Stop him! *(*YUN *steps aside.* KU, *act-* *ing as* YUN, *intercepts the man from* SOLMAE.*)*

KU: Where are you going?

SOLMAE: I heard my kid ran away from home.

YUN: I asked what he was talking about as he didn't have any kids.

KU: Your kid? You don't have any children, do you?

SOLMAE: I mean the child of the House of Geese. She ran away.

YUN: *(Prompting* KU.*)* "But she's not the House of Geese's kid, is she? I know all about it." You see, I was trying to pressure him.

KU: But she's not really the child of the House of Geese, is she? You put her up for adoption when she came along, didn't you? I know all about it!

(The SOLMAE *leper collapses to the ground as if someone had kicked him in* *the stomach. From the ground he bows twice and murmurs the following speech* *while rubbing his hands together, still wearing red plastic gloves. His mur-* *muring is such that it is not clear whether he is speaking or weeping.)*

SOLMAE: Please forgive me! We only wanted her to live a normal life. To live like a normal person. I did it—a damned leper, living in hell—I did it, and I wasn't afraid of god at all.

YUN: "But it's not just the one kid," I said. "It's all the children." I bullied him—said that if he really wanted to see his children have a normal life, he should just disappear, burn his house down, and go far away.

KU: *(Acting as* YUN, *addresses the leper.)* You've got to leave the children alone. Only if you leave them alone can they live like ordinary people. Listen to me. Set your house on fire and leave town tonight.

YUN: As I was speaking, I saw a red flame from the direction of Solmae.

(In the distance, the night sky grows red.)

KU: What's that fire? Isn't that your house?

SOLMAE: Oh, my lord! My wife! Get out of there! You've got to get out! Please forgive me. Oh, no. What am I going to do?

(Clutching at the air, he disappears into the darkness.)

KU: What's that fire all about? Who set the fire?

YUN: I was going to get the girl, so I turned my bike around.

KU: I said, who set the house on fire?

YUN: I knew we would lose the girl for good if I didn't catch her. So I rode back on the bike. Turn the bike around.

KU: Was it the girl—the girl from the House of Geese who set the fire?

YUN: As soon as I turned the bike around, I heard a woman's voice.

*(*KU *parks the bike and sits on it. The feeble voice of a woman is heard from a distance.)*

VOICE OF THE WIFE FROM SOLMAE: Yŏn-ji! Where are you? It's me. Yŏn-ji! Hey, where are you? It's me!

KU: Who's that?

YUN: Put out the lights, please.

VOICE OF THE WIFE FROM SOLMAE: Yŏn-ji! Hey! It's me!

YUN: Put out the lights!

*(*YUN *pulls the candles off the bicycle and stamps them out. The sky over Solmae glows red like a sunset.* YUN *is struck by something and falls to the ground, letting out a sharp scream. The red flames in the sky over Solmae die down rapidly, and the sounds of a cowbell and the galloping of a cow continue in complete darkness. The sound resembles that of rocks rolling. It recedes into the distance. Silence.)*

*(*KU *strikes a match to light a candle from the candle box.* YUN *straightens up.)*

KU: So what happened?

YUN: I passed out. Later they found my bicycle hanging on a branch of the pine tree down there. A whole boxful of burnt matches was spread around on the ground like a spider's web. And where the lines of matches were broken, I was lying with my arms and legs spread-eagled.——So, can you guess what it was?

KU: *(Pause.)* Could it be a cow? A cow, maybe, went by?

YUN: But was it that cow?

KU: Well, there was a cowbell and the sound of hoofbeats. So we can say that you were struck by a cow—that makes the story more believable. But that's different from your first report. Before, you said that you were stopped by a ghost—a woman calling you.

YUN: That's right! That's what I think I heard. But I don't remember anything else except that something hit me from behind. Now I wonder if it was a cow that hit me. You see, if it was a cow, I would have got over it in just a couple of days, but I was sick for a long time. I'd sit staring into space. I'd feel fine one moment, then suddenly my heart would start racing. It felt like I was possessed by something.

KU: Well, old friend, why don't you lie down again?

YUN: Lie down here?

KU: Let's see if we can hear what might have happened that night again. Maybe someone else can tell us a different story.

YUN: Who do you mean?

KU: You said you heard a voice, a woman's voice looking for the child. And without thinking, you put out the candles to see who it was. Right then you were hit by the cow . . . and while you were unconscious maybe the woman came here to see you. Let's see if this gets us anywhere.

YUN: You're right. The woman could have come here. She must have spotted me by the candlelight.

KU: Lie down here. Now, you're unconscious.

(YUN lies down. As if a film were being rewound and then replayed, the situation that occurred just before Yun blew out the candles resumes. The night sky glows red in the far distance.)

YUN: What's that fire? Isn't that your house?

SOLMAE: Oh, my lord! My wife! Get out of there! You've got to come out! Please forgive me. Oh, no. What am I going to do? (*Grasping the air, he disappears into the darkness.*)

(YUN *turns the bike around and rides on it. In the distance, the feeble voice of a woman is heard.*)

VOICE OF THE WIFE FROM SOLMAE: Yŏn-ji! Where are you? It's me! Yŏn-ji! Hey, where are you? It's me!

(YUN *pulls the candles from the wheel and stamps them out. The sound of rocks falling is heard in the darkness. The sound turns into the hoofbeats of a cow. The sound of a cowbell is heard. After a while, someone carefully breaks a pine branch, as if to see what effect the sound might produce. After the sound of breaking branches has been heard several times, footsteps are heard walking on the dried branches. It is the* WIFE *of the Solmae leper. She looks like her husband, although her leprotic symptoms are more advanced than his. She moves slowly and is so tiny that she looks like the second-eldest daughter of the House of Geese. She notices* YUN, *shakes him, and lights a match to look closely at the ground. She picks up the candles* YUN *had put out and relights them. She swings the candles in all directions as if wanting to let people know where she is rather than to look about the area. She speaks to herself, but loudly enough to be heard from a distance.*)

WIFE: Yŏn-ji-ya! Go home. Don't you see the fire? The fire! Your mother's house is on fire. I'm leaving, I can't stay here. Don't you see, sweetheart? It's bad to run away from home. You won't survive away from your home. Do you see the fire? Mommy can't come back again. Please, go home. You've got to listen to me. Your mother at the House of Geese will be looking for you. Don't run away, go home. Yŏn-ji-ya! Take good care of the little ones and don't tell them about me. Even if it means dying, never tell them about me. A sickness like mine doesn't give me much time. I won't come back to you. Don't worry, and go home. Don't run away, my little baby!

(*She flashes the lighted candles in all directions in an act of cleansing the area, then extinguishes them with a bowing motion. She disappears as if she had been sucked into the dark. The rustling sound of her plastic garment lingers for quite a while and then stops abruptly. Silence. The red sky over Solmae rapidly darkens.* KU *comes out and* YUN *sits up straight.)*

YUN: The wife of the Solmae leper died that night in the town hospital. Severe burns, they said.

KU: Hush! Someone's coming. Lie back down!

(YUN *lies down and* KU *hides himself. From the direction in which the* WIFE *from Solmae disappeared comes the sound of men exchanging whispers. Soon, the* OWNER *of the Persimmon-Tree House and his* SERVANT *appear. The* SERVANT *stumbles over* YUN's *body and falls down.)*

SERVANT: Ouch! What's this? (*The* OWNER *of the Persimmon House lights a match.*) Isn't that Yun, the town clerk? Oh my, he must have been kicked by a cow.

OWNER: Nonsense. He's only drunk. Must've passed out from too much to drink.

SERVANT: (*Lights a match to see the cow footprints.*) The cow ran this way, I'm pretty sure.

OWNER: It'll run all night long. Come on, let's go.

SERVANT: What should we do with this guy?

OWNER: Don't worry about it. He'll make it home after he wakes up.

(*The two men quickly disappear into the dark.*)

KU: Who are those people?

YUN: They're from Persimmon-Tree House. (*Pause.*) "I was in bed for forty-two days after being hit by a cow." But I should have some injuries, don't you see? Some open wounds or broken bones, something like that. It's maddening because I don't have any of those.

(*He puts his arms around his chest.*)

KU: When did you wake up after passing out?

YUN: Not till the next day at home. Hwang—the wine maker—found me and brought me home.

KU: Hold on, aren't you skipping something here?

YUN: (*Pause.*) Well, no, I . . . don't think I missed anything.

KU: What about the sound of the young woman?

YUN: The young woman?

KU: Yeah! You said the young woman followed you from the begin-

ning. As I see it, seems like you felt this woman hanging around
you till you saw the fire at the Solmae house, and then all of a
sudden she vanished. Let's go back to the beginning. Let's trace
what happened step by step. Stop me if I leave anything out or if
you remember something. *(Takes out the draft of the absence report
from his pocket.)* This is your absence report. You fainted one night
because the ghost of a young woman called out to you from a
hidden grave. A young woman who was recently buried at the
side of a road is the one who appears in your report. Then, you
met a second woman: the young woman of the House of Geese.

The House of Geese

(Suddenly, the loud sound of geese is heard inside the fence. The YOUNG
WOMAN *appears.)*

YOUNG WOMAN: I sent my sister away.

YUN: What do you mean, "sent her away"?

YOUNG WOMAN: Last year they brought us a newborn baby from the
house across the way.

YUN: The house across the way? You mean . . . from the lepers?

KU: And you ask her if the girl who ran away was also from the lepers' house. Then, she asks you the same question.

YOUNG WOMAN: She came along when I was six. I don't know.
(Suddenly.) Did she come from there, too?

YUN: I asked you that question.

YOUNG WOMAN: In my dream, I . . . I . . . I set fire to that house. In a
dream . . .

YUN: Are you all right? Is she all right now?

KU: When the Solmae house was burning, wouldn't it be natural
to think of the young woman as you watched the fire?

Shintŭlmae Gully

KU: So, in Shintŭlmae Gully, you hear a woman's voice following
you. Later it turns out to be the wife of the Solmae leper. But

since you could only *hear* the voice, you might have thought it was the young woman from the House of Geese. Let's go over the part where you lit the candles to calm the little girl down— when she was riding on the back of your bike.

(YUN *lights the candles and puts them on the bike. The* CHILD *sits on the rear rack of the bicycle.*)

YUN: There was a big war a long time ago. A soldier was coming home from battle after winning the war. He rode a bike with Korean flags on each side. They say he shouted, "I am coming home! I come home alive!" Well, now you're riding with candles instead of flags. So why don't you yell like the soldier? "I'm coming home! I'm coming back home!"

(At *this moment the* CHILD *lets out a shriek, jumps down from the bicycle, and starts pulling it backwards as if she were in a rope-pulling contest. The* SOLMAE *leper appears.*)

YUN: Where are you going?

SOLMAE: My kid ran away from home.

YUN: Your kid? You don't have any children, do you?

SOLMAE: I mean the child of the House of Geese.

YUN: But she's not really the child of the House of Geese, is she? I know all about it! You put all of your children up for adoption, including the oldest and the newborn.

SOLMAE: Please forgive me. I only wanted to see them live like normal people.

YUN: If you want to see them live a normal life, you've got to go away. Burn your house down and disappear.

(The *fire at the Solmae House flames up.*)

SOLMAE: Oh, my lord! My wife! Please get out! (SOLMAE *exits.*)

YUN: (Abruptly.) I went there to tell him to burn the house and disappear.

KU: Went where?

YUN: Over to Solmae.

KU: But when did you go? Did you follow him?

YUN: No.

KU: Was it after the cow hit you?

YUN: I don't remember. But I'm sure I went over there.

KU: And?

YUN: I found the young woman there. She was there.

THE HOUSE AT SOLMAE

(A small hut is on fire. The hut is only the size of a cow shed with its roof hanging so low that it nearly touches the ground. The YOUNG WOMAN *is crying and screaming on the ground. Then, in an effort to put out the fire, she repeatedly approaches the house and then retreats.)*

YOUNG WOMAN: Mama! *Aigoo!* Mama! Oh my god, fire! What are you doing? Mama! Get out of there. No, no, my mama's burning to death—why's there no sound? Mama! Oh my god! I'm killing my mother. I set the fire. Yes. I lit it to burn your disease away. To heal you, Mama. To burn everything and to heal. *Aigoo!* Mother, I only did it 'cause I was afraid. What are you doing? Mama, get out of there. Now we can live together. I'll take you in. But you've got to get out of there. What's she doing in there? She's burning to death! My mother's dying. Get out quick, or you'll die. What am I gonna do? I started the fire. *Aigoo!* Mama! *Aigoo!* Mama! I killed my mother! What can I do? My own mother! My mother!

(The YOUNG WOMAN *freezes. The flame freezes. Like an auditory hallucination, a voice calling the names of people is heard. A picture of a crowd of people who died in the registry building fire is projected on the screen of flames.)*

VOICE OF A NORTH KOREAN SOLDIER: Pak Pyŏng-hun, Sŏng Ki-man, Yu Sŏk-jun, Ch'oe Hŭi-bok, Cho Chun-gŏl, Kim Yŏung-sŏp, Kim Chae-il, Yi Pang-hŭi, Yi Won-baek, Yi Pang-jin, Chang Tong-su, Kim Ch'ŏn-ŭi, Pak Sang-sŏk, Yu Sun-hŏn, Yi Pyŏng-jun, Yi Yŏng-hwan, Cho Chŏng-do, Pak Chung-won, Shin Sŏng-u, Hŏ Sŏng-sŏk, Ch'oe Ch'ang-hwan, Im Hong-sun, Pak Sŏng-gon, Kim Myŏng-hak, Kim Yŏng-gyun, Yi Su-wung, Chŏng Ch'a-ryang, Yi Chŏng-il, Im Tae-ch'ŏl, Song Hong-gu, Yi Kŏn-ch'ŏl, Yi

Si-bok, Chŏng Kwang-il, Ch'ŏn Tu-sŏk, Hyŭn Ch'ang-uk, Yun Chŏng-p'il, Yi Chong-baek, Yi Sang-dae, Yi Nae-won, Kim In-gwan, Chŏng Chin-gŏl, Chŏng Chin-yŏng, Hŏ Kwang-mun, Shim Kŭn-sŏk, Hwang Hon-yŏn, Chŏng Kwang-su, Chŏng Kwang-yi, Yi Sang-lae, Ŏm Chŏng-won, Mun Paek-hyŏn, Chang Kŭm-yong, Yun Chŏng-t'ae, Yun Chŏng-mok.

Yun Chŏng-mok! Set the fire, get your bag, and follow us!

(Yun's UNCLE, *who has been sitting in one corner of the stage, breaks a glass bowl into pieces. He picks up a piece of glass and cuts his forehead.)*

UNCLE: I set the fire! Yes. I did it! Please, let this living man live!

VOICE OF A NORTH KOREAN SOLDIER: Kim Chung-gil, Pak Sang-sun, So Nam-sun, Cho Yŏng-ho, Ch'oe Yŏng-bin, Yi Sŏng-gyun, Shim Hui-jun, Chang Kŭm-yong, Chang Kŭm-yŏp, Ch'oe Chŏng-yŏn, Hŏ Kwang-gu, Sŏng Hong-gyŏng, Kim Hak-su, Yu Ŭi-hwan, Kim Won-man, Kim Tong-ch'ŏl, Yu Kyŏng-sŏk, Yi Pang-jae, Pyon Yŏng-hwan, Kim Chun-hoe, Kim In-shik, Pak Chae-hwan, Shin Kyu-jŏng, Yi Nam-hŭi, Yi Wu-kyŏng, Kim Chung-gi, An Chong-ch'ŏl, Cho Yang-il, Hong Chong-ok, Chu Chong-gŭn, Yi Yong-gil, So Ki-yŏng, No Chŏng-yun, Pyŏn Yŏng-hun, Yi Pan-bok, Chŏng Yŏng-il, Kim Won-p'yŏng, Hŏ Hyŏk, Ch'oe T'ae-hwa, Yi Chun-nam, Yi In-jae, Won Chŏng-guk.

So Kwan-ho! Set the fire, pick up your bag, and follow us.

(SO KWAN-HO, *who has been sitting in another corner of the stage, breaks a glass bowl into pieces. He picks up a piece of glass and cuts his forehead.)*

SO KWAN-HO: I set the fire! Yes. I did it! Please, let this living man live!

VOICE OF A NORTH KOREAN SOLDIER: Kim Wi-sŏng, Kim Su-hwang, Kwon T'ae-mu, Kang Si-jin, An Yŏng-sang, Ch'ŏn Kil-bŏn, Cho Kyŏng-su, Chŏng U-bok, Yi Chae-gŭn, Yang T'ae-o, Shin Yong-gil, Pae Su-byŏng, Ko Sŏng-jin, An Ŭi-gyŏng, Shin Chong-guk, Cho Po-gŭn, Yi Chin-ho, Mun Paek-sŏn.

(Everything stops. Everything turns to the color of ashes.)

Yun, a clerk of the town registry office, falls ill after encountering a ghost of a young woman.

Town Registry Office

YUN *and* KU.

KU: *(Reading a draft of the absence report.)* On the eighth of last month, on my way home after working the night shift, I passed out in Shintŭlmae Gully where I was run over by a three-year-old cow. I recovered the next day, but the severe headache, along with high fever and loss of consciousness, made it impossible for me to work. Whereupon I submit this report of absence. Respectfully, Yun Chin.

(The lights fade.)

INTIMACY BETWEEN
FATHER AND SON

Cast of Characters

KING YŎNGJO

SEJA, *the Crown Prince*

QUEEN CHŎNG-SUN, *Yŏngjo's lawful wife*

LADY SŎN-HŬI, *Yŏngjo's consort and Seja's mother*

LADY HONG, *Seja's wife*

PING-AE, *a lady attendant*

POK-YE, *a lady attendant*

EUNUCH

KU SŎN-BOK, *a military official*

HONG IN-HAN, *a courtier*

SONG MYŎNG-HŬM, *a royal official*

YI SŎK-MUN, *a royal official*

IM TŎK-JE, *a historian*

NARRATOR

(The stage is built in two storeys; the upper-rear level represents KING YŎNGJO's *palace, while the lower level represents* SEJA's. *At the center of the upper stage is a royal seat for* YŎNGJO. *There is an entrance at each side of the upper level. The upper stage is also connected to the lower stage by a ramp, stage left, and a staircase, stage right. Underneath the upper stage, at the rear of the lower level, is a hidden space divided into three sections, covered by white screens. This space allows for swift entrances and exits of the actors and serves as a storage space for properties such as the rice chest and puppets. At the center of the lower-stage floor*

is a bright-yellow square mat, which is SEJA's *space. The play is performed without interruption. Actions often take place simultaneously on both the lower and
upper levels, or scenes flow into each other with only a short lapse of time. Thus,
indications of scenic locations do not necessarily imply formal scene divisions. Two
musicians sit in the stage-right corner, and a* NARRATOR *sits in the stage-left
corner on the lower-level floor near the audience. As spectators enter the theater,
they see* LADY HONG *in a white mask sitting in the stage-right corner of the upper
stage. Indeed, she sits there, holding her son (a puppet) in her arms, throughout
most of the performance. A vignette precedes the actual beginning of the play, in
which* SEJA *and four courtiers perform a lively dance. At the sound of court music
signaling the entrance of the king,* SEJA *and the courtiers freeze for a moment;
then the courtiers exit.*)

Yŏngjo's Private Quarters

(YŏNGJO *enters from the right-corner entrance and* LADY SŎN-HŬI *and*
QUEEN CHŎNG-SUN *from the left-corner entrance of the upper level.*
YŏNGJO *sits behind a paper screen. In front of the screen sits* QUEEN
CHŎNG-SUN, *who, at the age of fifteen, is tiny and childlike.* LADY SŎN-HŬI
stands near the QUEEN.)

NARRATOR: *(Reading from* LADY HONG's *journal.)* May fourth, the thir-
ty-fifth year of the reign of King Yŏngjo. The nation's three-year
mourning period for the death of Queen In-wŏn having concluded, the Board of Ceremonies appealed to his Majesty to take
as his lawful queen the daughter of Kim Han-gu, he of the
Kyŏngju clan. Thereupon, a state wedding was duly celebrated
in June. The bride was Queen Chŏng-sun. The age of his Majesty
was sixty-six years; that of Queen Chŏng-sun was fifteen.

YŏNGJO: Whose daughter is this?

LADY SŎN-HŬI: She is the daughter of Kim Han-gu of the Kyŏngju
clan. She is fifteen years old.

YŏNGJO: Lift your head. I want to see your face. *(To* LADY SŎN-HŬI.)
What is your opinion?

LADY SŎN-HŬI: Since the funeral ceremonies of the two queens are concluded, it is appropriate to proceed with the royal wedding.

YŎNGJO: I shall leave it to you to take care of the necessary details.

LADY SŎN-HŬI: I will see to it that everything is performed with the greatest care.

(*With a slight lift of* YŎNGJO's *finger, the screen is rolled up. A balmy, youthful smile spreads across his sixty-six-year-old wrinkled face.*)

SEJA'S PALACE

(*The lower stage. Summoned by* YŎNGJO, SEJA *prepares to put on regal attire with the help of a lady attendant,* PING-AE, *and the* EUNUCH. *In one corner, the* EUNUCH *prostrates himself on the floor waiting for* SEJA *to finish dressing.* SEJA *suffers from a chronic illness called "clothing disease," which makes wearing heavy clothing painful. He moves and twists his body in tortured anguish as he attempts to put on his formal regalia.*)

SEJA: (*Blurts out carelessly.*) Sixty-six and fifteen. That makes her fifty-one years younger. Fifteen and sixty-six. That makes him fifty-one years older. Younger or older, the difference is still fifty-one. Is that not so, Eunuch?

EUNUCH: That is correct, Your Highness. (*Not wanting to put on his clothing,* SEJA *feigns preoccupation with something else.*) I fear that His Majesty may lose his temper because you are taking so long.

YŎNGJO'S PRIVATE QUARTERS

(*On the upper stage* QUEEN CHŎNG-SUN *is sitting on* YŎNGJO's *lap.*)

YŎNGJO: (*Taking off the* QUEEN's *sock, caressing her, and giggling.*) Let me see your foot. (*Bites it.*)

QUEEN: (*Screams.*) Ah!

YŎNGJO: (*Abruptly yells.*) Why on earth doesn't Seja come! I told him to come immediately. Why is he taking so long?

(*On the lower stage,* PING-AE *struggles with* SEJA *while attempting to dress him.* PING-AE *makes desperate efforts to coax him into wearing his clothes,*

attempting to desensitize his back by whipping it with a long white cloth. SEJA
groans in pain but smiles. Yet each time PING-AE *tries to clothe* SEJA, *he slips
out of his robe. It is clear that* SEJA *wants to wear the robe, but his will cannot overcome an inner compulsion. When* PING-AE *finally succeeds in getting
the robe on* SEJA, *he savagely removes it.*)

SEJA: Wait! What is this? Turn it inside out. What is it?

PING-AE: I don't see anything, Your Highness.

SEJA: Let me see. What is this?

PING-AE: I am afraid it is just small strands—

SEJA: Strands . . . ?

PING-AE: *(Apologetic.)* Strands of thread.

SEJA: Strands of thread. This is what has been crawling on my skin.
   (Throws the robe down.) Take it away!

PING-AE: *(Bringing other clothing.)* You need to raise your arm, Your
   Highness.

SEJA: Wait a minute.

   (SEJA *struggles with himself for a minute and finally raises his arm. Relieved,*
   PING-AE *opens up the sleeve so that he can push his arm through.*)

SEJA: *(Abruptly.)* Wait! I feel it again.

PING-AE: But I see nothing.

SEJA: Yes, that's it! It is the hair on my skin that prickles. *(Plucking
   body hair from his arm.)* Now I feel nothing. I am ready.

PING-AE: *(As if to a child.)* Please, put your left arm into this . . .

SEJA: And put my right arm he-re. Wait! *(Pulling his arm back from the
   sleeve, he starts scratching his leg.)*

PING-AE: Let *me* see to this, Your Highness. Just remain still.

SEJA: What are you going to do?

PING-AE: Raise your left arm, Your Highness.

SEJA: *(Angrily.)* No, no! What is all this bustling about? *(Lamenting.)*
   Why does it trouble me so? Give it to me. *(He yanks the robe from*
   PING-AE *and tears it into pieces.)* This is a curse! Someone must have
   cast a spell on me in order to destroy me.

EUNUCH: I am afraid that your tardiness will anger His Majesty.

   (On the upper stage, QUEEN CHŎNG-SUN *exits, leaving* YŎNGJO *alone.)*

SEJA: Ever since I was a boy, it has been difficult—irritating—to wear clothing. Now it has gone far beyond that. It is simply impossible for me to wear these robes. It is not just my mind; this cursed body refuses to obey me.

YŎNGJO: *(From upper level.)* Is there no sign of the prince yet? *(Incensed.)* Why does it take him so long to dress?

(On the lower stage, PING-AE quickly brings out new regalia. SEJA takes a deep breath and stretches his arms out straight. PING-AE starts to put the new clothing on SEJA, but again he refuses. SEJA's whole body writhes in torment. Frustrated and enraged at his own illness, SEJA violently strikes PING-AE with a long stick. PING-AE rolls on the floor in pain, her hands clutching her back. Sensing that his life may be at stake, the EUNUCH quickly picks up the stick that SEJA has dropped and falls on his knees.)

EUNUCH: I have an idea! Place this stick on your shoulders, behind your neck, and hold both ends with your hands to prevent it from falling.

SEJA: *(Follows the EUNUCH's instruction.)* Just like a prisoner receiving his just punishment.

EUNUCH: Please, do not allow the stick to drop, Your Highness.

SEJA: See here, I might very well drop it. You must tie my wrists to it.

EUNUCH: Good heavens! Please take that order back.

SEJA: *(Speaking to himself.)* Scandalous . . . horrifying.

(YŎNGJO appears on the ramp that leads to the lower stage and watches SEJA for a while. SEJA and his attendants are not aware of the king's presence.)

SEJA: I said go ahead and tie my hands.

(SEJA spreads his arms, and the EUNUCH reluctantly ties SEJA's wrists to the stick that crosses behind SEJA's neck. Looking like a scarecrow, SEJA kneels down and waits for his attendant to dress him. SEJA suddenly senses his father's presence. Caught in this awkward position, he hurriedly greets YŎNGJO by prostrating himself on the ground.)

YŎNGJO: *(Cold and sarcastic.)* I hear that you have been ill. But from your conduct now, I see that your illness is hardly fatal. *(To EUNUCH.)* How long has it been since father and son last met?

EUNUCH: It has been about two months.

YŎNGJO: *(To the prince).* But where in heaven's name have you been? Have you been wandering about the palace? I hear that you have

been seeing a serving maid, even as we mourned your grandmother's death. Is it true that you have been seeing a servant?
(Pause.) You are worse than a beast to do such a thing during the
mourning period. Who is this servant, Eunuch?

EUNUCH: Please do not ask me to betray two masters, Your Majesty.
I would rather die.

YŎNGJO: Call in the girl! *(YŎNGJO exits. PING-AE, who has turned deathly
pale, falls on her knees.)*

PING-AE: Please, take my life! *(Starts to go.)*

SEJA: You shall not go! Just sit there. *(PING-AE stops.)*

EUNUCH: But His Majesty's order is as hard as stone.

SEJA: Leave that to me.

EUNUCH: Please be sensible.

   (SEJA draws a sword that has been lying in one corner of the lower stage.)

SEJA: Say no more or I will cut your throat. Go back and report
what you have seen and heard.

   (The EUNUCH, petrified, exits.)

PING-AE: Please let me go. You are courting disaster—and all because of a servant like me? Since this lowly servant received your
grace, there is no more reason to live.

SEJA: Even if you wished to live, would they let you? *(Nervous laugh.)*
Death will come faster for me than for you. *(Serious.)* But I will
not sit back waiting for it to strike.

PING-AE: Where are you going?

SEJA: I will enter the upper palace through the water-passage.
(Raises his sword high in the air.)

PING-AE: Your Highness, please kill me before you leave.

   *(SEJA rushes to the upper stage and strikes his sword on the royal seat. But, as
   if repelled by some unknown force, SEJA falters back and exits.)*

SEJA'S PALACE: PRIVATE QUARTERS

*(On the upper stage, LADY HONG continues to sit in the right-hand corner
with SEJA's son in her arms. She wears a flat, white mask devoid of features.*

The EUNUCH, *with a ghastly look on his face, enters the lower stage carrying a clay pot in which medicines have been prepared.)*

EUNUCH: *(While squeezing medicine from a cloth into the pot, he reports to* LADY HONG.*)* Severe orders for the capture of Ping-ae are coming down from the king's quarters like stinging raindrops. But Seja rejects His Majesty's commands, threatens people with his sword, and orders them all to leave. Before this row gets completely out of hand, I must replace Ping-ae with some other serving girl. As it happens, there is another maid who is about the same age as Ping-ae. *(Calls to backstage.)* Pok-ye!

*(*POK-YE *is a young maid in her early twenties with a slender face. She is a happy-go-lucky girl, completely ignorant of palace intrigues and therefore unaware of her doom.)*

POK-YE: *(Chatters upon entering. She speaks in a crude and rapid dialect.)* I'm here, I'm here. I've just been laying down—that snack made me sicker than a dog. There were tons of goodies left over from the king's wedding, you see. Guess I had way too much, though. Anyway, what d'you need me for?

EUNUCH: *(Gravely.)* Do you remember the day when the Crown Prince killed Kim Han-ch'ae, the eunuch?

POK-YE: *(Trying to make her description as realistic as possible.)* With one good swipe. Blood gushed out—spread all over the place, like a mountain covered with red flowers.

EUNUCH: On that very same day, you accompanied the prince to T'ongmyŏng Hall where the mourning altar for the late queen rests.

POK-YE: *(Utterly shocked.)* Accompanied? What did you say? The Crown Prince?

EUNUCH: That is precisely what you must tell His Majesty when he interrogates you.

POK-YE: *(Innocently.)* Phew! You're talking nonsense. *(Suddenly she realizes the gravity of the conversation.)* I swear on my own life, I never did such a thing!

EUNUCH: There at T'ongmyŏng Hall—you became one with the prince.

POK-YE: *(Trying to imagine the idea of sleeping with the prince.)* There
I became one with the prince? *(Giggles.)* Oh my! That's embar-
rassing!

(To cool her face, POK-YE *fans herself with her sleeve. The screen rolls up,
revealing* LADY HONG. *The* EUNUCH *picks up the clay pot and pours the medicine into a bowl.* POK-YE *prostrates herself before* LADY HONG.*)*

POK-YE: *(Crawling toward* LADY HONG.*)* This lowly servant never did
such a thing. Even if you kill me, I swear I didn't. *(Desperately cries
for help.)* Your Highness! Your Highness!

*(*LADY HONG *remains silent, signaling her rejection of* POK-YE's *plea by raising her right arm.)*

EUNUCH: With the exception of the day the state funeral for the
departed queen was held there, you accompanied the prince
every day to T'ongmyŏng Hall. All you have to say is those two
phrases. Say no more than that.

POK-YE: But I can't!

EUNUCH: Do you wish to die at once?

POK-YE: *(Sternly.)* Kill me, I still did no such thing. *(After a pause,* POK-
YE *holds up the medicine bowl. She looks at the bowl and takes a deep breath.
Unable to bring the bowl to her lips, she knocks it over and weeps softly.)* Yes.
I accompanied His Highness. *(The* EUNUCH *weeps along with* POK-YE.
She crawls closer to LADY HONG *and makes a deep bow. Accepting her fate,
calmly.)* I slept with the Crown Prince.

*(*POK-YE *exits, shortly after which her scream is heard. An attendant's voice,
loudly announcing the death of the Minister Min Paek-sam, overlaps the
sound of* POK YE's *screaming.)*

VOICE OF AN ATTENDANT: The Minister of the Right, Min Paek-sam,
has just taken his own life!

EUNUCH: *(Wailing.)* No! It was only a few days ago that the prime
minister, Yi Ch'ŏn-bo, died. What a disaster for His Highness! It
means that the Crown Prince has now lost his most loyal sup-
porters; they were like his own arms and legs.

(At this moment, LADY HONG *loses her composure. The* EUNUCH *holds her
by the arm and cries bitterly.)*

EUNUCH: My lady!

THE COURTYARD

(At the king's command, the courtier HONG IN-HAN *and the royal army officer* KU SŎN-BOK *are drafting an edict for the deposition of Prince* SEJA.*)*

HONG IN-HAN: What words can make it clear that Prince Seja's violence has gone beyond the bounds of simple human error?

KU SŎN-BOK: Just say "violent rampages"—it's as simple as that.

HONG IN-HAN: But in writing the edict we need to take into account his status as Crown Prince.

KU SŎN-BOK: But we're in the middle of deposing him, aren't we?

(The courtiers YI SŎK-MUN *and* SONG MYŎNG-HŬM *enter hurriedly.)*

SONG MYŎNG-HŬM: We have heard that you are drafting an edict of deposition. Is that true?

YI SŎK-MUN: Put it away! His Majesty's anger has subsided since they executed the maid.

KU SŎN-BOK: This is an important affair of state. Do you think His Majesty would order us to draft this just because of a maid?

HONG IN-HAN: But is it not true that His Majesty has recently calmed down and become more circumspect in his behavior toward the prince?

KU SŎN-BOK: All this talk is useless. "His lawless violence having effected such disastrous consequences, the following actions are taken."

(Pause.)

SONG MYŎNG-HŬM: I am deeply at fault as I failed to guide His Highness along the correct path. Now that you are writing the edict of deposition, how can I ever turn my face toward heaven? I shall return home and end my life.

YI SŎK-MUN: But you must not forsake His Highness.

HONG IN-HAN: How can I dare say that I serve the people?

KU SŎN-BOK: Cut all these wordy phrases. Just say we must depose him because he has gone mad. And have done with it.

HONG IN-HAN: We have already said "violent rampages." What else do you think should be added here?

KU SŎN-BOK: But what I say is the truth, isn't it?

SONG MYŎNG-HŬM: You must stop your slander. You are an officer in the royal army and must conduct yourself accordingly.

HONG IN-HAN: Why don't you write it, sir?

KU SŎN-BOK: Look!

(HONG IN-HAN *takes off his cap.* KU SŎN-BOK *picks up a sword that* YŎNGJO *has given him.*)

YI SŎK-MUN: How insolent are you! Do you know where you are?

KU SŎN-BOK: I am executing the king's command.

(YI SŎK-MUN *and* SONG MYŎNG-HŬM *bow at the mention of the king's command.* HONG IN-HAN *puts his cap back on and resumes writing with his brush.* YŎNGJO *enters.* KU SŎN-BOK *hands the sword to* YŎNGJO. SEJA *enters.* HONG IN-HAN *reads the deposition edict.*)

HONG IN-HAN: I hereby deliver His Majesty's edict concerning the deposition of the Crown Prince. Royal subjects, see to it that his order is carried out scrupulously.

"The violent rampages of Prince Seja are unprecedented. To insure the health of the state, I have undertaken all possible measures to cure his madness. Only parental indulgence prevented me from taking sanctions against him. Nevertheless, his insane violence has reached a point where it will surely bring disaster on the state. Having paid due homage at our ancestral shrine, we therefore declare that the Crown Prince is henceforth deposed of his royal rank and status.

"Who can possibly understand my predicament—either from the inside or the outside? Here I hand over a piece of writing. Promulgate an edict. But, ah, his violent rampages have tormented me day and night, burdened me with fear for the state and our people. For my own part, he and I are bound by the human relationship of father and son. I wonder what has gone wrong to drive this situation beyond our control."

(YŎNGJO *and* SEJA *have entered the lower stage. During the reading of the edict,* YŎNGJO *squats in one corner, repeatedly tapping the floor with his sword in a stabbing motion.* SEJA *prostrates himself a few feet behind him. Both* YŎNGJO *and* SEJA *face toward the audience.* YŎNGJO *severely rebukes* SEJA.)

YŎNGJO: Take off your coronet and robe!

(SEJA *hurriedly takes off his regalia. Now stripped down to his undergarment, he looks small and slender like a woman. It is a hot summer day. The sun is unbearably hot.* YŎNGJO, *still stabbing the ground with his sword, severely reprimands him.*)

YŎNGJO: You have committed a crime for which you must die. Die at once!

SEJA: *(In sober earnest.)* I know I have committed many crimes, but I do not know for which crime I must die.

YŎNGJO: How dare you attempt to hide your crimes! You shall die immediately!

SEJA: At your command, I will obey and die at once. But permit me to take my life outside the palace grounds.

(*The royal officials* YI SŎK-MUN *and* SONG MYŎNG-HŬM *enter, confronting military guards who block the gate. They shout at guards, who are invisible onstage.*)

YI SŎK-MUN: But this is a crisis of state! Why do you bar the way of royal officials? Step aside now.

SONG MYŎNG-HŬM: His Highness's life is at stake. How dare you shut the gate in such a crisis? Get away!

YI SŎK-MUN: If His Majesty asks who allowed us in, tell him it was I, Yi Sŏk-mun.

(YŎNGJO *intervenes, and the two subjects prostrate themselves at the sight of the king.*)

YI *and* SONG: Your Majesty!

YŎNGJO: *(To the unseen guards.)* Why have you allowed these scoundrels to enter!

SONG MYŎNG-HŬM: Even the evil tyrant, Qin Shi, did not commit the crime of filicide, Your Majesty.[1] Why do you attempt to kill your own son?

(YŎNGJO *strikes at* SONG MYŎNG-HŬM *with his sword, but* SONG MYŎNG-HŬM *manages to avoid the blow and runs away.* YŎNGJO *hands the sword to* YI SŎK-MUN, *who remains petrified with fear.*)

YŎNGJO: *(To* YI SŎK-MUN.*)* Follow that man. If he enters another man's house, cut him down, and the owner of the house as well.

But if he goes straight to his own home, just make a show of wounding him. If he is willing to die by his own hand, then let him live. But if he attempts to save his life by making excuses, cut his throat and bring me his head!

(Unable to disobey the order, YI SŎK-MUN *exits, following* SONG MYŎNG-HŬM.*)*

SONG MYŎNG-HŬM'S HOUSE

*(*YI SŎK-MUN, *carrying the sword, follows* SONG MYŎNG-HŬM *on the ramp, stage left.)*

SONG MYŎNG-HŬM: I do not intend to live if His Majesty orders me to die. Only allow me a moment to pay homage at the shrine of my ancestors.

*(*YI SŎK-MUN *allows him to do so.* SONG MYŎNG-HŬM *makes a deep bow at his ancestral shrine and another deep bow toward the royal palace.)*

SONG MYŎNG-HŬM: *(Speaking as though the king can hear him.)* A king and his subject, a father and his son, embody a fabric of human kinship that is woven in heaven and bound on earth. Your Majesty, the Crown Prince does not know the reason for his death, yet you relentlessly insist that he die. Your servant shall die as you have commanded. But I humbly pray that, with my death, His Royal Highness shall be spared.

*(*YI SŎK-MUN *raises the sword high.* SONG MYŎNG-HŬM *stretches his neck forward to receive the blow. But* YI SŎK-MUN *lowers the sword and goes away.)*

SONG MYŎNG-HŬM: *(Bewildered.)* Why do you not kill me?

YI SŎK-MUN: His Majesty said that if you were prepared to die I should spare you.

SONG MYŎNG-HŬM: Ah, His Majesty's whims are so wayward that I do indeed fear for Seja's life. *(Outraged.)* His Majesty is playing a joke on his subjects. Why does he speak in double meanings? *(Snatches the sword from* YI SŎK-MUN *and attempts to strike his own heart with it.* YI SŎK-MUN *stops him.)*

YI SŎK-MUN: But we know that this is simply part of his nature. It is not our place to take umbrage. Seja will be saved once again—if only he behaves well.

THE COURTYARD

(On the lower stage, SEJA *is in the midst of a violent spasm. He groans in pain, rolling and twisting his body on the ground.* QUEEN CHŎNG-SUN'*s voice is heard offstage, singing a children's song.* YŎNGJO *starts to walk up the stairs to the upper stage following the sound of the* QUEEN. *When* YŎNGJO *is halfway up the stairs,* SEJA *emits a painful moan.* YŎNGJO *turns back and shudders at the sight of* SEJA. *The king runs to the prince and embraces him. The following speech is quoted from* YŎNGJO'*s decree for the deposition of the Crown Prince.)*

HONG IN-HAN: "Ah! Even at this advanced age and with this gray hair, I have nevertheless brought forth havoc unparalleled in the history of the state. How can I say that I serve the state and its people, let alone honor the rituals of my ancestors? Why should I not eliminate him if they say he has gone mad? But even as I write these words, tears fall on my robes."

*(*SEJA *clings to his father like a child while* YŎNGJO *continues to embrace him. This rare moment of tenderness between father and son is soon interrupted when* QUEEN CHŎNG-SUN *enters from the upper-level stage.* YŎNGJO *immediately detaches himself from his son and turns his attention to her.)*

QUEEN: *(Impudently.)* Your Majesty! *(Walks down the stairs to the lower stage.)*

YŎNGJO: Oh! *(Indulgently to the* QUEEN.*)* What ceremonies are planned for today?

(The QUEEN *recites the names of ritual games while leading* YŎNGJO *across the stage to the ramp and up to the king's private quarters.* YŎNGJO *lies on his stomach while the* QUEEN *massages his back with her buttocks.* YŎNGJO *enjoys the massage, smiling lasciviously. Meanwhile,* SEJA *has followed* YŎNGJO *and kneels near* YŎNGJO *and his wife. The prince then senses the onset of another seizure. He clenches his fists, grits his teeth, and trembles violently in an attempt to control his mounting rage. After a few seconds, he loses control and*

lets out a horrible scream. The QUEEN *screams back in terror and runs to the rear of the stage.* YŎNGJO *follows her with his arms stretched wide, protecting her from his mad son.* SEJA *rolls on his back in an uncontrollable convulsion. The* QUEEN *exits screaming.* YŎNGJO *returns to his royal seat, beside himself with anger.* SEJA *falls back to the lower stage. His convulsion slowly subsides.)*

YŎNGJO: *(Looking at* SEJA *on the lower stage.)* I am told that you dug a dungeon in which you keep funeral clothing and weapons. For what purpose?

SEJA: *(Barely collecting himself, but earnestly.)* For no particular purpose. I simply could not discard them, because I could not recover from the late queen's death. I hid them there, fearing you might see them. If you send someone there to look for them, you will see I am telling the truth.

YŎNGJO: Show me what you did in the dungeon.

(Courtiers bring out funeral clothing and weapons on a cartlike altar. Also on it are a paring knife and a cucumber. Upon seeing these objects, SEJA *becomes deeply sad. His actions are so frivolous, however, that he nevertheless looks as if he is mocking* YŎNGJO.*)*

SEJA: Please do not do this to me. Don't. Your humble servant feels only unbearable pain inside.

YŎNGJO: I hear that you dressed yourself in funeral robes, cursing me each night in your dungeon. Do exactly what you did, but this time in front of me!

SEJA: *(Cries out to the late Queen Chŏng-song,* YŎNGJO*'s former wife.)* Mother Chŏng-song! *(Pause.)* I understand that Your Majesty insists on my death. I do not know for what crime I am being punished, but I realize I have no other choice. Thus I will kill myself to fulfill Your Majesty's wish. But since I must not sully your worthy presence with such a horrible, unclean death, I will leave the palace to kill myself.

YŎNGJO: Listen to him! Listen to what he says—instead of following my orders! Do you dare deceive me? When you ask to leave the palace, whose protection are you seeking? If you do not kill yourself, I will die first. *(Taking off his robe, he rushes to the lower stage.)*

SEJA: Your Majesty! Please, don't!

(YŎNGJO *feigns striking himself with a sword—obviously a vain gesture. The royal subjects restrain him.* SEJA *also tries to stop him by grabbing the sword.*)

YŎNGJO: (*Face-to-face with* SEJA *over the sword.*) Should I die or should you? If I die, our three-hundred-year dynasty will end. If you die, the dynasty can be preserved. I cannot let it perish at the cost of preserving your life!

(YŎNGJO *attempts to strike* SEJA *with the sword. But the blow is blocked by royal officials. The sword whizzes past* SEJA's *head.*)

SEJA: My soul is so terrified that it has already left my body. I understand now that Your Majesty truly desires my death. I will not disobey.

(*Belying his words,* SEJA *clings to his father, begging for his life.*)

YŎNGJO: (*Returning to the royal seat upstairs.*) Show me the curse you put upon me in the dungeon. Let me see what you did there. Show me exactly what takes place in your dungeon.

SEJA: (*To royal officials.*) Assist me.

(*Sunlight has been pouring down in intense heat—so hot that it can bake a brick. With the help of royal officials,* SEJA *dons funeral clothing. As soon as he is dressed, a red curtain covers the stage, which then becomes* SEJA's *dungeon at T'ongmyŏng Hall. Weapons placed here and there educe a mood of bloodthirstiness. An ancestral tablet is set up. In one corner,* PING-AE *stands, wearing white Buddhist clerical attire as if she were going to perform a Buddhist dance. Instead,* PING-AE *and* SEJA *start a dance that is quite frivolous and sensuous. The dancing ends as abruptly as it started. In this scene,* SEJA *imitates his father's behavior with the* QUEEN.)

SEJA: Is there anything that I cannot do?

PING-AE: There's no such thing, Your Highness.

SEJA: You are wrong. Remove your clothing. (*She takes off her peaked hat. Her head is shaven.*) There are two things I cannot mend. One is having a twenty-eight-year-old son stricken by a mortal disease.

PING-AE: What kind of disease is it?

SEJA: It is a murdering disease. Since the year of his coming of age, this monster began murdering people. He has killed eunuchs and attendants; he has killed so many people that we have lost count. (*Chuckles.*) One time he slew an attendant in the service of his own mother, Lady Sŏn-hŭi. On another occasion, he dragged in a blind man from the street and ordered him to read his fortune. When the blind man said something wrong, they threw his dead body from the palace. He has killed court physicians, fortune-tellers, countless servants. . . . Good heavens, not a day goes by that corpses are not removed from the palace. No one knows who the next victim will be. The whole court is panic-stricken. I can no longer let this monster live!

PING-AE: But you've killed only a handful of servants. What can they do to you? Your Highness, you are heaven.

SEJA: You are mistaken. Take off your robe.

(PING-AE *takes off her clerical robe and is now wearing only an undergarment.*)

SEJA: How old are you?

PING-AE: Twenty-eight.

SEJA: That's my son's age.

(SEJA *chuckles.* PING-AE *giggles along with him.* SEJA *weeps.* PING-AE *comforts him. Recoiling from her,* SEJA *walks upstage. He places a sword on his stomach and bitterly wails.*)

SEJA: I have a son to kill, stricken by an evil disease. But if I kill this beast, I will need another son. And that means I must father another. But I am too old to sire any more sons. A sad state of affairs. (*To* PING-AE.) Come closer. Come here, don't stop.

(*Instead of moving closer to* SEJA, PING-AE *pulls down her underwear. With the paring knife* SEJA *peels the skin of a cucumber and places the cucumber in his mouth.* PING-AE *kneels on her hands and knees.* SEJA *kneels behind* PING-AE *and gyrates the cucumber several feet behind her in a sexual fashion. She moves her hips in sympathetic response, but then falls forward to the ground as the cucumber falls out of* SEJA's *mouth, symbolic of unsuccessful penetration. She nervously giggles, almost weeping, as she fiercely attempts to save her life.* SEJA *chuckles. He turns the sharp blade of the sword toward* PING-AE. *When it approaches her body, she falls back over the funeral altar. The royal officials shout and pull the altar back into the hidden space underneath the upper stage. All of a sudden, the point of the sword is directed toward* YŎNGJO. *Under the glaring sunlight,* SEJA *twirls the sword, having completely lost his mind. Royal officials rush onto the stage.)*

YI SŎK-MUN: What is all this about, my lord? The palaces of king and prince lie apart from each other: it is only natural that a word or two has been misconstrued between them. Perhaps a simple misunderstanding. How can Your Majesty wreak such havoc based on the words of one woman?

SONG MYŎNG-HŬM: Even though Seja has lost his virtue, may not Your Majesty still care for him with benevolence and love? Why not give His Highness another chance to repent and understand his transgressions?

HONG IN-HAN: Even if you felt it necessary to reprimand His Highness, you should have brought him before the throne to rebuke him. Your Majesty, the sight of His Highness kneeling under the blazing sun is most cruel.

YŎNGJO: Say no more! You are all dismissed!

SEJA: At least allow me a method other than by my own hand. A sword, a cup of poison, anything but that.

SONG MYŎNG-HŬM: Even though Your Majesty has just relieved me of my duties, I will never leave the palace, even if you destroy me.

YŎNGJO: Do you all wish to be banished?

YI SŎK-MUN: Your Majesty first needs to question those who are blackmailing His Highness and discover their hidden motives. Since this incident is unprecedented in our long history, I entreat Your Majesty to calm your raging storm and find remedies by consulting your royal kinsmen and subjects.

YŎNGJO: What you are saying is all very true, no doubt, but too late. Dismiss all of them from their offices. Take them away, now!

(The historian IM TŎK-JE *enters, yelling.)*

IM TŎK-JE: *(To the guards.)* You ignorant knaves! I am a historian! As the royal chronicler, I cannot miss such a grave incident, even for a second. I will keep my post even if you kill me. As long as I have pen and ink in my hand, you dare not drive me out.

YŎNGJO: Take him out and execute him at once. *(Exits.)*

(As the palace guards attempt to take IM TŎK-JE *out,* SEJA *tries to stop them. A struggle with the guards ensues.)*

SEJA: He must not go! I will never let go of him: you may as well chop off my arm.

IM TŎK-JE: *(Being dragged off by his arms.)* Your Highness, this is beyond my poor powers. Please forgive me. *(A shriek comes from backstage.)*

SEJA: *(Left alone on the stage, dejected.)* Where are you going? Why are all of you deserting me?

*(*SEJA *takes off his funeral clothing and pulls out the rope drawstrings that cinch the waist and cuffs of his pants. He attempts to strangle himself with one rope, but his action begs for intervention. Four officials enter, carrying small drums. They take the rope from him.* SEJA *attempts to strangle himself with a second rope, but again the officials intervene. As the action is repeated, it gradually evolves into a dance, with* SEJA *and the royal officials dancing vigorously to musical accompaniment. The stage becomes a playground for* SEJA*'s amusement. Within the commotion of loud music and rapid dancing, a* PHYSICIAN *sneaks in with a bowl of medicine. He provides* SEJA *with a drink to help him regain energy—an action that catches the attention of* YŎNGJO, *who appears behind the screen upstairs.)*

YŎNGJO: You blockheads! *(Runs down the ramp to the lower floor.)* How dare you allow such a thing! *(Gives his sword to* YI SŎK-MUN.*)* Dismiss Han Kwang-jo from his post on the Board of Medicine, and chop off the head of Doctor Pang immediately!

(While YI SŎK-MUN *is getting ready to behead the* PHYSICIAN, SONG MYŎNG-HŬM *comes forward.)*

SONG MYŎNG-HŬM: The physician only did what I told him to do. Let it be my fault, not his. I humbly ask that you execute me in his place.

YŎNGJO: *(Granting* SONG MYŎNG-HŬM*'s wish.)* Then slit that villain's throat at once!

*(*YI SŎK-MUN *makes* SONG MYŎNG-HŬM *kneel down in one corner.)*

YI SŎK-MUN: I know you did not commit a crime, but it is His Majesty's wish that you be executed. His Majesty's command shall be fulfilled. Prepare to die.

(Wields the sword but cuts only the topknot of SONG MYŎNG-HŬM*'s hair.* YI

sŏk-mun *then presents the topknot to* yŏngjo.)

YI sŏk-mun: My swordsmanship is so clumsy that I could not cut his head off. Since I committed the unforgivable crime of not fulfilling your command, I entreat you to kill me.

yŏngjo: Stupid rascal, don't you even know how to swing a sword? For this I will deal with you later!

(Despite his vengeful words, the king appears to be pleased by his subject's loyalty to his colleague. He roars with laughter while exiting up the ramp to the upper stage. After yŏngjo *leaves,* song myŏng-hŭm *brings the bowl of medicine to* seja.)

seja: *(Much relieved.)* While His Majesty is gone, hide me somewhere in the palace gardens. Please take me there.

YI sŏk-mun: Your Highness, you should not go anywhere at present. I know His Majesty's commands are stern today, but if you can bear with them everything will be all right. That is how the ways of heaven and of man work. It will be better for you to remain calm and follow His Majesty's words. For His Majesty is heaven, and there is no way for Your Highness to avoid the will of heaven.

(Comforted by YI sŏk-mun, seja *starts playing games. He pulls out a deck of cards and plays a card game with the royal officials.)*

seja: What you say is true. I will gladly follow your instructions. But can I ask you one favor?

song myŏng-hŭm: What is it?

seja: I want to see my son. Could you bring him to me?

song myŏng-hŭm: *(Hesitant for a moment, but soon reassuring.)* I will do my best. Take care of yourself. *(Exits.)*

YI sŏk-mun: Why does Your Highness not wear the coronet? Please put it back on now.

seja: I may not wear it any longer—His Majesty ordered me not to.

YI sŏk-mun: But I am worried that such an unruly appearance will bring forth even more disasters.

seja: Will I be able to avoid disaster if I wear the coronet?

officials: *(Together.)* We are afraid for Your Highness.

(With the royal officials' assistance, seja *puts on his coronet and robe. He*

appears to have fully recovered his sanity. SEJA *and the royal officials start to perform a dance called* Ch'unaeng mu. *It is an elegant and stately court dance suggesting* SEJA's *calm and peaceful state of mind. In this dance,* SEJA *looks dignified and regal. But this peaceful moment is soon interrupted, as the ghost of* POK-YE, *the maid executed in place of Ping-ae, enters from the hidden space. She covers her head and torso with a shawl, but one can see numerous puppets tied on to her body. The legs of the puppets hang out from under her shawl.)*

SEJA: *(Notices* POK-YE *and stops dancing.)* Who's that?

*(*POK-YE *twirls without answering.* SEJA *pushes the shawl back from her head, revealing a brutally misshapen* POK-YE *with her eyeballs missing and half of her face crushed.)*

SEJA: *(Taking several steps backwards.)* Who are you?

POK-YE: I am Ping-ae who accompanied Your Highness to T'ongmyŏng Hall.

SEJA: Ping-ae?

YI SŎK-MUN: An evil specter! How dare you appear in our midst. Begone!

SEJA: Did you say you accompanied me?

*(*POK-YE *spins round and round.)*

SEJA: What have you done to my Ping-ae? Who are you who claims to be she? Whose attendant are you?

POK-YE: I am Ping-ae who accompanied Your Highness to T'ongmyŏng Hall.

*(*SEJA *removes her shawl. His violent madness seizes him once again.)*

SEJA: Someone is playing a ghastly trick on me. She never accompanied me. This is humiliating—that they thought I could be scared off by the sight of a mere servant girl. I will cut off your head and send it back to them!

*(*SEJA *takes the sword and hacks at her.* POK-YE *spins round and round. Puppets fly from her body and are scattered all over the stage.* SEJA *goes to each puppet and stabs it with his sword. All the courtiers except one have already left the stage.* SEJA *runs to the upper stage and strikes the empty royal seat numerous times.)*

SEJA: *(Shouts.)* Do you hear? It is the voice of thunder!

OFFICIAL: Thunder does not speak when the sun is so bright.

SEJA: *(Relapsing into his madness, yells out.)* What inspires more terror than a king? *(Pause.)* What can disgrace a king? It is I who bring shame to His Majesty. The sound of thunder is more terrifying than the king. Do you hear it? The voice of thunder! Thunder! *(Walks down the stairs to the lower stage.)* I feel strange. I must say farewell to my son. Bring the grand heir to me. *(He looks around to find that all the royal officials have left. Frightened, he speaks to POK-YE.)* Do you see? Do you see the magpies floating above T'ongmyŏng Hall?[2] *(POK-YE smiles, showing her teeth.)* Go to T'ongmyŏng Hall and look closely at the crossbeam. If you hear the beam crack, run away as quickly as possible. Someone is approaching. Go, now. Fly there like a deadly magpie.

(POK-YE passes him by, spinning round and round. The sound of magpies approaches. As if bringing the sound of the birds with her, LADY SŎN-HŬI, Seja's mother, enters. She looks grotesque, her lower body enormously swollen. This character is played by a man standing in a large barrel supported by wheels. She slowly rolls down the ramp to the lower stage.)

SEJA: *(Sits down on the stairs.)* Mother!

LADY SŎN-HŬI: How are you feeling?

SEJA: I think I shall die soon. Those black-winged creatures are in high spirits today—surely they will take me away soon.

LADY SŎN-HŬI: Please get hold of yourself.

SEJA: *(Yells.)* Why is the grand heir not coming?

(LADY SŎN-HŬI suddenly lifts her arms and swings them in the air as if shooing away birds. She carelessly strolls around like a sleepwalker and speaks the following lines loudly, as if attempting to memorize them from a book. YŎNGJO enters upstage and listens to her.)

LADY SŎN-HŬI: *(To the imaginary birds.)* Shoo, shoo! Go away! You need not cry over this. I have already decided to leave him to his fate. Go away! The number of people which Seja has killed approaches one hundred. It includes eunuchs, attendants, and officials. I cannot even count how many crimes he has committed. His debaucheries continue day and night, as his servants constantly escort girls—even monks—to the palace. He even

violated a serving girl who belonged to me. Once he dug a grave
in front of T'ongmyŏng Hall and attempted to bury an attendant alive after performing inconceivable acts. On that same
day, His Majesty left the palace to pray for rain. I mumbled to
myself that if it rained within three days His Majesty would be
safe, but that if it did not rain, Seja would have his will. When it
rained, I could barely calm my trembling heart. His Majesty is in
grave danger. And when the king's safety is threatened, I can no
longer be bound by the personal feelings of a mother for her
son. I could not help but report what I know to His Majesty. I
have dared to come here because I can no longer sit waiting to
see what will happen. *(Moves closer to the stairs where* SEJA *is sitting and
confronts her son face-to-face.)*

SEJA: *(Incredulous.)* Mother! *(Comes down the stairs and looks into her face.)*
Mother! *(*LADY SŎN-HŬI *turns her back on him.)* What has happened
to you? *(Desperately embracing his mother.)* Have you gone mad?

LADY SŎN-HŬI: Do not resent my decision too much. It was more
important to protect the grand heir than to save the heir appar-
ent.

*(*LADY SŎN-HŬI *sinks into the barrel which, without her upper torso, looks like
a giant bell.* SEJA *is now completely lost and has no one to whom he can turn.
He rolls on the floor, both crying and laughing.* SONG MYŎNG-HŬM *brings
the puppet representing the grand heir.)*

SEJA: *(Stretching his arms toward his son.)* My baby! *(Even before* SEJA *can
take a good look at his child,* YŎNGJO *enters, yelling indignantly.)*

YŎNGJO: You, guard, take the grand heir outside.

SEJA: *(Resigned, self-scorning.)* I do not recognize my parents. Could I
even recognize my own son? Take him away.

YŎNGJO: Take him outside, quickly. *(Changes his mind.)* No, give him
to me.

SEJA: No! *(But* SONG MYŎNG-HŬM *hands the baby to* YŎNGJO.*)*

YŎNGJO: *(Carrying his grandson on his back, he walks up to the royal seat on
the upper level.)* Everybody out! Men-at-arms, make sure no one is
allowed inside. If anyone disobeys, I will slaughter him on the spot.

(SEJA *falls down unconscious. The military chief,* KU SŎN-BOK, *enters, followed by four courtiers.* LADY HONG *also appears on the upper stage.*)

KU SŎN-BOK: There is not one subject in the entire country willing to strangle His Highness. Even if His Highness attempts to strangle himself, your subjects would rather untie the cord than pull it. And it will be so even when ten years have passed. Bring out the rice chest!

(*From the hidden space, military guards bring a large, empty rice chest onto the stage.*)

YŎNGJO: Do you mean that I must put him inside?

KU SŎN-BOK: Please order His Highness to enter the rice chest of his own volition. If that is not possible, command us to carry out the task.

(SEJA *suddenly straightens up. He sees the rice chest, then looks at* YŎNGJO, KU SŎN-BOK, *and finally at his mother,* LADY SŎN-HŬI. *He looks inside the rice chest and then listens to the sound of magpies. In one corner,* LADY HONG *stands like a shadow wearing a mask.*)

SEJA: (*Runs to the upper level via the ramp and kneels down, imploringly.*) Father, father! I have done wrong. I will do what you have always wanted me to do. I will study. I will do whatever you command. But please do not force me to do this!

YŎNGJO: If you cannot enter by yourself, shall I command these guards to carry you in?

SEJA: (*After a pause.*) Anyway, why should I want to live? (*He mumbles the following speech to his wife,* LADY HONG.) Something will happen to me, I know, but what am I supposed to do? Why have events spun out of control like this? He loves the grand heir. So long as he has his grand heir, he does not care if I am gone. The grand heir is my own son. But I and my son have different fates. What can I do? You will see. You and your children will be all right. It is only I who suffer from this disease. I feel strange. No matter what happens, do not be alarmed and be prepared for it.

YŎNGJO: (*To military guards.*) Take Seja's eunuch Pak P'il-su, his female companions, his servants and shamans—take everyone

out of the room who has ever been close to this beast and execute them all.

(KU SŎN-BOK *exits. Resigned to his fate,* SEJA *stands in front of the rice chest.*)

SEJA: Assist me. (*A soldier kneels down so that* SEJA *can step on his back to get into the chest. He looks at* LADY HONG *and speaks enigmatically.*) I will look after you. (*He stares at her for a moment and moves his lips slightly as if to speak something to her. He disappears into the chest.*)

YŎNGJO: Pound in the nails!

(*Blackout. When the lights come back on, they shine only through the hidden space of the entire downstage wall, exposing piles of puppets that represent Seja's innocent victims. From this space, military guards wearing butcher's aprons remove the bodies of the victims with large hooks and toss them into the rice chest. The guards wear bloodstained black aprons and carry the corpses in ritualized dance movements. The lights change, indicating that several days have passed.* YŎNGJO, *who has gone backstage during this scene, reenters wearing a simplified, modern version of a black regal robe. He carries the grandson-puppet on his back.*)

YŎNGJO: (*To* SEJA *in the chest.*) Do you know how many days have passed? (SEJA *sticks his hands out from the rice chest and makes the sign of seven.*) Seven days! Yes! Keep on! You said you could bear with it, so endure. Persevere. We must see it through to the bitter end. Why are you so afraid of thunder? Thunder is nothing unless lightning strikes you. Cover your ears and close your eyes tight. No, better yet, shout! Cry out at the top of your lungs, louder even than the thunder! Come, follow me. Do as I do. You monster! You kept funeral robes and weapons in your dungeon. Tell me why.

SEJA: (*Inside the chest, loudly beating a brass pot that was put inside with him as a chamber pot.*) Thunder! The voice of thunder!

YŎNGJO: On this sunny day, there is no thunder, you weakling. You want to kill yourself outside the palace? Do you think you will be rescued? (*Walking around the rice chest.*) Should I die or should you? If I die, the three-hundred-year dynasty will end, but——

SEJA: (*Retorts from the chest.*) If you die, our dynasty will be preserved. You bastard! Our dynasty will be preserved!

(*Upon hearing* SEJA*'s retort,* YŎNGJO, *violently enraged, thrusts his sword repeatedly through the chest.*)

YŎNGJO: Cover the chest with dirt!

(*Court soldiers cover the rice chest with more corpses. The sun blazes.*)

YŎNGJO: (*Panting.*) Should I die, or should you? If I die, the three-hundred-year dynasty will end, but—

SEJA: (*Retorts again.*) If you die, our dynasty will be preserved. You monster! Our dynasty will be preserved. So die then.

YŎNGJO: (*Jumps up and down on the chest in anger.*) Should I die or should you? If I die, the three-hundred-year dynasty will end, but—

(SEJA *is silent.*)

YŎNGJO: (*Hoping, in part, to hear his son's response, whispers into the chest.*) If I die, the three-hundred-year dynasty will end, but if you die, our dynasty will be preserved. You monster! Our dynasty will be preserved.

(SEJA *is silent.* YŎNGJO *realizes that he has finished his statement without* SEJA*'s interruption.*)

YŎNGJO: (*Whispers into the chest.*) If I die, the three-hundred-year dynasty will end, but . . . but . . . if you die, our dynasty will be preserved.

(*He finally realizes that his son has died. He hastily unties his grandson from his back and holds him tightly to his chest.*)

NARRATOR: (*From* LADY HONG*'s journal.*) May twentieth, in the thirty-eighth year of Yŏngjo. Around four o'clock in the afternoon, a torrential rain poured down and was accompanied by a prodigious crack of thunder. I cannot describe how deeply worried I was, for I knew that he was afraid of the thunder. I should have followed him unto death to avoid bearing witness to these events. But I could not follow him, because my duty lay with the grand heir. I could only grieve over the monstrous fate that joined us.

(*During this narration,* LADY HONG *approaches the king who is standing near the rice chest. She takes out a dagger in order to strike herself, but she cannot bring herself to do so. Instead, she slowly makes a deep bow to* YŎNGJO. *Lights slowly dim on the face of* YŎNGJO, *who stares blankly into space.*)

YŎNGJO: (*To* LADY HONG.) It has been difficult seeing you. Nonetheless, you took good care of the grand heir and brought him back to me.[3] I am grateful to you.

(*Blackout.*)

NOTES

1. *Qin Shi huangdi,* first emperor of the Qin dynasty in China (221–206 B.C.), was described as a cruel tyrant, famous for burning books and burying Confucians.

2. *Magpies* are a symbol of death in Korean lore.

3. *Nonetheless, you took good care of the grand heir and brought him back to me.* Lady Hong did indeed raise the grand heir well. As King Chŏngjo, he inherited the kingdom and proved to be one of Korea's greatest rulers. Chŏngjo also proved himself a loyal son: on ascending the throne, he restored his father's royal status and executed officials responsible for his death. It was Chŏngjo who asked his mother, Lady Hong, to write the journal that provided Oh with source material for the play.

"Let me see your foot!" Yŏngjo fondles his new wife.

Lady Hong, Seja's wife, with the grand heir.

Seja's convulsion.

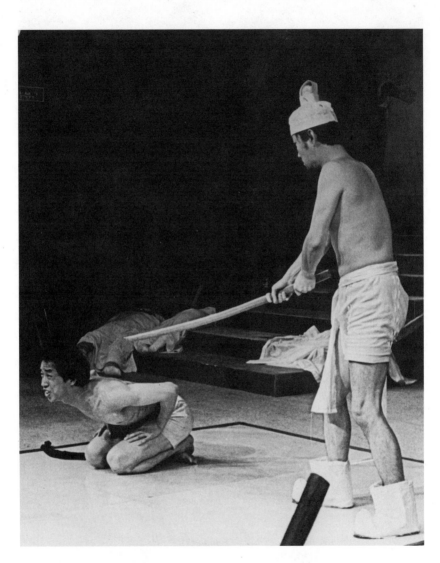

"Should I die or should you? If I die, the three-hundred-year dynasty will end, but if you die, our dynasty will be preserved." Yŏngjo threatens to kill his son.

A moment of sexual pleasure quickly turns fatally violent for the serving maid Ping-ae.

Seja "voluntarily" walks into the rice chest.

CH'UN-P'UNG'S WIFE

Cast of Characters

ACT ONE

(YI CHI *and* TŎK-JUNG *enter pushing the* FATHER *and* SON *before them. The hands of the* FATHER *and* SON *are bound with rope.*)

FATHER: What is this? We've been walking up and down the seashore, getting nowhere. Didn't you say we're going to Seoul?

YI CHI: But you said Seoul was on the water.

FATHER: This is the East Sea. The water that goes around Seoul is the Han River.

TŎK-JUNG: This water, that water—I give up. My legs hurt. Hey, Yi Chi, why don't we let these crooks go and take off on our own?

FATHER: Now you're talking! It'll take us months to get to Seoul.

Forget Seoul. Why don't you guys hold the trial right here and let at least one of us go free? There's more than twenty people—our wives and children—depending on us, you know. Kill one, if you have to, but let at least one of us go back home. *(Wipes tears away with his sleeve.)*

TŎK-JUNG: All right. The court is in session!

YI CHI: Now what do you know about a trial, you stupid ass? You can't even read.

TŎK-JUNG: Well, if there's something we need to know, we can ask these guys as we go along. Hey, how do you begin a trial anyway?

FATHER: Well, now, the two of us, father and son, look just like the crooks on this wanted poster. The police in Seoul are offering a hundred bucks for us. We supposedly sold silver to these little Japanese bastards—strictly prohibited, you know. In other words, we're what you call smugglers.

*(*TŎK-JUNG *unfolds a scroll on which the portraits of the alleged criminals are painted.)*

YI CHI: So, between the two of you, who's the brains behind this scheme?

SON: I am. I got the government official to set us up in business with the damn Japanese dealers.

FATHER: No, that's not true! I'm the brains. I delivered the silver to the official when he brought in lots of expensive cloth to pay for it.

TŎK-JUNG: Well, I guess that makes both of you the brains, then. What'll we do with them, Yi Chi?

SON: Well, my father may have delivered the silver, but I came up with the idea. So, I'm in charge of the operation. My father was only following orders.

FATHER: Look here, the silver belonged to my family. It may have been my son's idea, but he wouldn't have even thought about stealing the silver without my say-so. It only makes sense that I am the brains and my son's the accomplice.

YI CHI: Then, according to you, neither of you guys is guilty. The son's innocent because he cut the deal following his dad's orders. And the father isn't guilty because all he did was hand over the silver as part of his son's racket.

TŎK-JUNG: That's right! You're proven innocent of this crime. The father's innocent because he's a stooge. His son's innocent because he's only a flunky.

YI CHI: Cut the ropes and let'em go!

TŎK-JUNG: Okay, okay! This feels good! Now, get the hell out of here!

(As TŎK-JUNG *is about to untie the ropes, the* WIFE *enters.)*

WIFE: You idiots are completely messing up the laws of the land. You stupid amphibians! You don't know the first thing about how people think. *Aigoo!* What am I supposed to do now? *(Suddenly squats down and wails.)*

TŎK-JUNG: Is this a man or a woman? God, she's ugly!

WIFE: I came all the way from Seoul to see you guys when I heard about your magic powers. But I've gone to all this trouble for nothing. *Aigoo,* what do I do now?

YI CHI: Well, can *you* tell which of these two is the brains of the outfit?

WIFE: Look, it's simple. According to the law, when there's more than one crook in a family, you punish the head of the house. The father is the brains, not the son. Don't you see how simple it is? Do you think a son can tell his father what to do? God, have I screwed up! Why did I come all this way to meet these assholes? *(Wails.)*

YI CHI: She's absolutely right!

*(*TŎK-JUNG *suddenly knocks his head against the* FATHER, *who falls backwards covering his eyes.)*

YI CHI: *(To* TŎK-JUNG.) Be careful. He'll go blind.

FATHER: He made me blind!

TŎK-JUNG: What do you need those eyes for, anyway? They're useless. You couldn't even see that your own son was a crook when they were working. Get him out of here!

SON: Wiser words were never spoken. *(Exits, dragging the* FATHER *behind him.)*

YI CHI: *(To* TŎK-JUNG.*)* What're we supposed to do now? There's only one solution—get some bug spray and commit suicide.

WIFE: Now what's the matter with you?

YI CHI: Look, we just set those guys free. Where are we going to get the hundred bucks we were promised for taking them to Seoul?

WIFE: What do you need the money for?

YI CHI: My mother—eighty years old—has been sick for three years now, deep down in the sea. One day, the doctor told us that *tŏdŏk* roots, which grow up here in the world, would cure her. Tŏk-jung's my cousin on my mother's side. We held a family meeting, and we two were chosen to come up here to find the roots. It's been a year now. A year ago we changed ourselves into human form and went up to Yŏngsanp'o.[1] But to this day, we don't even know what they look like, let alone how to find them. We got so frustrated we thought if we had some money, we could just buy the roots somewhere. But now there's no chance of that. I guess the only thing to do is kill ourselves.

WIFE: Why do you need so much money for *tŏdŏk* roots?

TŎK-JUNG: We hear they're expensive.

WIFE: Now, boys, listen to my story. I've made a lot of money from weaving cloth over the past three years. I made so much money that even the big millionaire, Sŏksung-i, is dying of jealousy. With all that money, my life should be perfect. But I have one problem—my husband left me, because I was born with a defect.

TŎK-JUNG: What's wrong with you? Do you have a split lip?

WIFE: I've got six fingers.

TŎK-JUNG: Let me see. Yah! That's a nice way of putting it. Your arm is all deformed.

WIFE: Don't tease me about my looks. Even though I look like this, my husband rarely notices other women.

YI CHI: What's his name?

WIFE: Ch'un-p'ung. Yi Ch'un-p'ung.

YI CHI: Where's he now?

WIFE: He scraped up all the money we had and went to

Pyongyang—to start a business, he said.[2] But he met Ch'u-wol, the famous Pyongyang courtesan, and took her as a second wife. He's completely lost his mind over her. Like time doesn't even exist for him. So, a month ago, I wrote him that his wife had kicked the bucket because of pent-up anger disease.[3]

TŎK-JUNG: What do you mean "kicked the bucket"?

WIFE: I mean I cut a cold fart.

TŎK-JUNG: Did it smell bad?

WIFE: Are you listening or what? The letter said that I had died and gone to the other world. Good grief! I see him coming this way. (*Rushes about madly, not knowing what to do. Suddenly flustered, she loses her vigorous spirit and starts limping.*) What should I do? If he finds out I lied to him and didn't die, he'll beat the shit out of me. Help me, please!

TŎK-JUNG: Squeeze your butthole tight so that the cold fart won't leak out.

WIFE: Squeeze tight. Then?

TŎK-JUNG: Pick up the bucket.

WIFE: What bucket?

TŎK-JUNG: Well, I don't know. Take off your shoe instead, and hold it tight.

WIFE: Hold my shoe tight.

(TŎK-JUNG *bumps the* WIFE *with his head and she falls backwards as though dead.* CH'UN-P'UNG *enters.*)

YI CHI: (*Pretending to dress the "deceased" for burial, wails.*) A poor, miserable woman was Ch'un-p'ung's wife! She could do anything, though, with a needle and thread. She'd make five pennies weaving, three pennies darning socks . . .

(*Seeing* YI CHI *dressing the "dead"* WIFE, CH'UN-P'UNG *wails sorrowfully.*)

CH'UN-P'UNG: Oh, no! Oh, no!

TŎK-JUNG: She'd earn two pennies mending old clothes.

CH'UN-P'UNG: Oh, no! Oh, no!

YI CHI: She worked day and night, year in and year out—dying cotton in the winter, spinning hemp in the summer, weaving it into cloth in the fall. And she saved every penny. And then, she loaned out her money, collecting interest daily and monthly until she wound up making a fortune.

CH'UN-P'UNG: Wait a minute, what are you saying?

TŎK-JUNG: I'm in the middle of giving a eulogy to the King of the Underworld. If you're going to butt in, do it in writing.

CH'UN-P'UNG: Don't you want to hear about my little darling— about how pretty my Ch'u-wol is? *(The following lines are delivered in a singing mode.)* She's fifteen. Just imagine her, sitting behind a half-drawn screen, wearing a beautiful green and red dress. She outshines the lovely sweetbrier and puts other legendary beauties to shame. When I'm with her, I forget all other pleasures. I forget music and the passage of time. All I have is Ch'u-wol. I want to hold her and keep her beside me. But to do it, I need that money. You've got to give it to me.

TŎK-JUNG: Whew! When you see a person lying on the ground like this, the least you could do is ask if she's all right, let alone have a little sympathy.

CH'UN-P'UNG: *(Ignoring* TŎK-JUNG.*)* I wound up a miserable beggar. I became Ch'u-wol's servant, fetching buckets of water up to her house. I just barely survive on the rice and a measly chunk of bean paste I get in a broken bowl. I really need that money. Give it to me!

(After hearing CH'UN-P'UNG's *story, the* WIFE *collects herself and sits up.)*

WIFE: What's that? Let me look at you! *(Cries, while checking out his appearance.)* What's happened to you? Where's your nice hat and all your accessories? You look horrible in those ragged clothes and that broken-down cap.

CH'UN-P'UNG: *(Irritated to see her, pushes her away.)* I left you at home with enough money to live in comfort with your three sons. What a mess you've got us into—you were lying on the street pretending to be a corpse just so you could look for me, weren't you?

WIFE: Well, yes. But don't you remember that I bought ten herrings with the money, that you gave me one and eight bits when you left?

CH'UN-P'UNG: So how are my three sons doing?

WIFE: The oldest one died—hit by a pinecone while sleeping under a tree.

(*At this news,* CH'UN-P'UNG *weeps mournfully.*)

WIFE: The second one drowned catching eels in the river.

(CH'UN-P'UNG *cries sorrowfully.*)

WIFE: The third one was lovely, but I'm afraid I pestered him so much that he died of convulsions.

(CH'UN-P'UNG *cries again and then in a rage suddenly swings his fist at the* WIFE, *who faints.*)

YI CHI: What the hell are you doing? I revived her so you could talk her out of her money.

CH'UN-P'UNG: What do I need money for if I'm childless?

TŎK-JUNG: But without money how can you see your Ch'u-wol again?

CH'UN-P'UNG: That's right! Doctor, doctor! Is there a doctor around here?

YI CHI: But a sudden attack like this is incurable.

CH'UN-P'UNG: Hey, you, blind man. Blind man!

FATHER: (*Feeling the way with a cane, enters.*) Who's calling me?

CH'UN-P'UNG: Here! Over here. Please recite a prayer to revive the dead.

FATHER: What's her family name?

CH'UN-P'UNG: Her name is Shim Tal-lae. The family name is Shim.

FATHER: (*After shaking small bells attached to the cane.*) O you Spirits of Heaven and Earth! Unfortunate is Shim Tal-lae . . . from Namsan, Seoul . . . in Korea . . . in the East Sea of the Rising Sun. Passed out in an accident, her life is hanging in the balance. Please be generous and merciful unto her. (*Shakes the small bells.*) (*Trying to think of something to say, he starts singing.*)

> *Look at the maiden in the field—*
> *What's that ribbon made of,*
> *Dangling at the end of your long hair?*
> *Is it silk or satin?—Ah, ha, ha, hei, hei, yo.*
> *What does it matter if it's silk or satin? —Ah, ha, ha, hei, hei, yo.*

CH'UN-P'UNG: Look here, are you done?

FATHER: She'll live again if you let me finish this prayer.

CH'UN-P'UNG: Well, how far are you from the end?

FATHER: I'm exactly halfway through the whole prayer.

CH'UN-P'UNG: Then go on.

FATHER: You need to pay.

CH'UN-P'UNG: How much?

FATHER: Exactly one hundred dollars.

CH'UN-P'UNG: I'd rather quit. Let's drop the whole thing.

FATHER: What? If you leave her like this, she'll wander back and forth between life and death. She'll keep coming back to bother you. What'll you do with her then?

CH'UN-P'UNG: But if I give you the hundred bucks, then what? I'd have to carry her half-dead body around on my back, and I'd still be broke. Forget it. I'll just bury her.

FATHER: Then why'd you get me recite a prayer in the first place? Why didn't you just let her go?

CH'UN-P'UNG: Now wait a minute. That woman may be ugly as sin, but she's still my wife. Go on! Fetch some singing pallbearers. We'll have to take her to the cemetery.

FATHER: Why bother carrying her all the way over there? Just bury her right here and be done with it.

CH'UN-P'UNG: But I haven't held a memorial service for my wife yet. What's done is done, I know. It can't be helped. I deserted her, but I'd still like to give her a really nice wake. *(Calls offstage.)* Hey, you! Pallbearers! Pallbearers!

(Three men in prison-guard uniforms enter immediately. They make formal bows, wailing as if at a funeral altar.)

GUARD 1: I am your son, killed by a pinecone. I'm here to fetch my father.

GUARD 2: I am your son, drowned while catching eels in the river. I'm here with my older brother.

GUARD 3: I am your son who died of convulsions. I'm here to follow my two older brothers.

(The three guards weep in a heart-wrenching manner. Suddenly, they jump on CH'UN-P'UNG *and try to carry him off.)*

CH'UN-P'UNG: *(Yelling.)* You idiots! I'm not dead, you ungrateful sons! Can't you see your mother's croaked, lying there cold as a stone? How come you're taking *me* away, instead of her? Are you trying to bury me alive?

GUARD I: No, we're going to Pyongyang.

CH'UN-P'UNG: What? You're Ch'u-wol's thugs, aren't you? That's it! Ch'u-wol must have gotten jealous when she found out I left her to see my wife. Aha!

GUARD I: The Inspector General of Pyongyang sent us to arrest you. You're charged with embezzling government money.

CH'UN-P'UNG: Holy shit! I'm finished.

(The three guards carry him out on their shoulders as if he were in a coffin.)

GUARDS: *(Singing a funeral dirge).* Is that Pukmang, I see, the Mountain of the Dead? Let us hurry there.

YI CHI: *(To the* FATHER.*)* Well, keep going. Finish the prayer.

FATHER: Oh, you'll need to pay a hundred bucks for that.

YI CHI: You'll get the money. Go ahead and revive her. Can't you see they're carting her husband away?

FATHER: *(After shaking the small bells vigorously.)*

> *Since all your kin and children,*
> *Lie prostrate at the burial service,*
> *Open your eyes once more, O Dead One.*

(As he recites this prayer, he unties the money bag from the WIFE*'s waist and puts it under his shirt. At this, the* WIFE *suddenly rises.)*

WIFE: Look at this guy! How come you're stealing my money, you thief. *(The* FATHER *hurriedly runs away.)* Well, what're you standing there for, you bastards! You in on this scheme too?

TŎK-JUNG: The old saying is never wrong. "Save a drowning man, and he'll accuse you of stealing his wallet." It's just the kind of thanks we get. That saying fits this situation to a T.

YI CHI: See here now, big sister. Forget your money bag. Think of it

as payment for your life and forget about it. Hey, do you think
you can still have a baby?

WIFE: What's a baby got to do with it?

YI CHI: If you could still do it, there's a way you could get a job in
the civil service. To save your husband, you really need a government post. But can you have a baby?

WIFE: Well, I think I can have one more.

YI CHI: Good! We'll get you a post.

WIFE: What do you mean, "good"? How in the world can I get pregnant without a husband?

TŎK-JUNG: I have a nephew who's got a big, strong post. Do you
think you could have a child with him? To get a government
job, all you need to do is have a baby.

WIFE: But I'd be too ashamed to see my husband afterward.

TŎK-JUNG: But all you'd see is the rotten face of his dead body.

YI CHI: Come on!

WIFE: But I can have only one more baby, just one!

TŎK-JUNG: Let's forget it then.

WIFE: You're mean.

YI CHI: Well, you gotta be ruthless to live.

(*Thunder strikes.* TŎK-JUNG *and* YI CHI *lie down on the ground and sing.*)

> *Turtle, turtle!*
> *Show your neck.*
> *Turtle, turtle!*
> *Show your neck.*

(*Thunder strikes. The* WIFE's *body writhes and jerks in synchronization with
the sound of thunder and lightning. She twists her body so violently that it looks
like the flame of a fire.*)

ACT TWO

(*The* WIFE *has secured a government position.* YI CHI *and* TŎK-JUNG *are
wearing headgear suggestive of their official status. In front of them, a young
couple [*HWA-JO *and the* SON] *is seated, tied up with rope.*)

YI CHI: Court is in session.

TŎK-JUNG: Young woman, you testify first.

HWA-JO: It was my mother-in-law's birthday. My husband brought home his mistress. He was having a grand old time with her, singing and dancing. I couldn't stand it, so I went to the bedroom and stayed in my bed, pulling the sheet over my head. Now he's pressing charges against me because of it. Claims I failed to observe proper etiquette—that I didn't offer a toast to her longevity. But I ask you, is it a crime for a girl to stay in bed?

SON: According to the *Kok-ye,* a man must leave his wife, even if he loves her, when his parents don't like her.[4] On the other hand, he must stay married if his parents wish him to, even though he hates his wife. That's the old rule, but my wife does everything she can to go against it. I just can't live with this woman.

WIFE: Do you have a dog in your house?

SON: We've got a yellow mutt big as a calf.

WIFE: A long time ago, a man named P'o-yŏng kicked his wife out of the house because she scolded their dog in the presence of his parents. Does your wife do things like that?

SON: Does she *scold* our dog? Are you kidding? She beats the living shit out of it.

WIFE: It would be perfectly all right to abandon your wife if it were still the old days. But times have changed. For instance, if you didn't have a dog in the first place, your wife wouldn't have offended your parents by beating it. You're more at fault than she is, since *you* were the one who kept the dog in the house on purpose, provoking her, knowing what would happen. In short, you're the real criminal. Take this lousy rat out of here and bust up his face. And send the woman back home, as she only played a small part in this business.

(TŎK-JUNG *knocks his head against the* SON, *who collapses on the ground clutching at his face. Shocked at this,* HWA-JO *weeps for him.*)

YI CHI: Hold on there, sister. What're you doing?

WIFE: I hate him for having a mistress.

YI CHI: Then why don't you do the same thing to your husband?

WIFE: Oh dear! I hadn't thought of that. What am I supposed to do now?

TŏK-JUNG: Don't worry. Next time just say, "Set the husband free and bash in the damn mistress's face." Then there won't be any problem.

WIFE: But how can I give completely different verdicts—saying "bust up his face" one time and "crush that bitch's face" the next—when it's really the same case? I got this post by giving up my very last child, and it's not as silly and meaningless a job as you think.

TŏK-JUNG: What are you talking about? The old saying goes, "Give a woman socks to walk on, and she'll make a pretty sash of them." A pair of socks belongs on your feet. And as long as you hold this office, you can say anything you like. At a time like this, why worry about such things as your reputation or whether your job means anything or not? Don't get so philosophical.

WIFE: Are you saying my post is a pair of socks? All right, then, I'll take them off for you. You can wear them. I don't want this job anymore.

TŏK-JUNG: Whoa! I don't know how to . . .

WIFE: What are you "Whoaing" about?

YI CHI: Look, we're in the courtyard of the Pyongyang government office. How can you forget about your husband so fast when he's sitting right in there with his head in the stocks?

WIFE: All right! I'll do what you tell me to do from now on.

CH'U-WOL: *(Enters with a wooden basket. Goes over to where* HWA-JO *and her husband are seated.)* Good lord! You must be starving. Here, drink some water. It'll make you feel better. *(Sees the* SON's *wounded face but thinks it is Ch'un-p'ung's.)* Oh my god! This bitch has murdered my husband. Good heavens, now I don't know what to do. You bitch, I'll get you for this even if I die doing it.

(She grabs HWA-JO *by her hair, and their two bodies, intertwined, roll on the ground.)*

WIFE: Is the bloodthirsty one his mistress?

TŎK-JUNG: That's Ch'u-wol, the notorious courtesan of Pyong-yang.

WIFE: God, she's ugly! She smells rotten too—no doubt from sleeping with this man and that man, day and night. She never washes, I suppose. She smells awful. Punch her ugly face in and bury her deep under ground. What a stench!

(TŎK-JUNG *mistakenly bumps his head against* HWA-JO *instead of* CH'U-WOL, *and she falls backwards clutching her face.*)

WIFE: What's the matter with you? Why did you crush that innocent woman to death?

TŎK-JUNG: Did I hit the wrong one?

WIFE: You must be blind to do that.

TŎK-JUNG: You said hit the ugly one. Are you saying Ch'u-wol looks worse than this one?

WIFE: That's your opinion.

YI CHI: I think I have to agree with my cousin.

WIFE: To me, she looks like a dead fish—she's got the face of a vicious ghost.

TŎK-JUNG: (*To* CH'U-WOL.) Look, you need to let Her Honor see your face up close. Come closer to her and make a bow. Her Honor is having difficulty seeing your face.

CH'U-WOL: Your Honor! I'm your humble servant, Ch'u-wol.

WIFE: That's your opinion.

CH'U-WOL: What?

YI CHI: Her Honor is asking, besides your face, what else you can present.

CH'U-WOL: I can sing a little bit.

YI CHI: Well, let's hear a song.

CH'U-WOL: (*In the traditional* p'ansori *singing mode*).

> *Let's go, if you wish to go,*
> *To places like*
> *So-gae, the best spot in Paek-ch'ŏn,*
> *Song-ch'ŏng, the best spot in Yŏn-an,*
> *Mu-ran, the best spot in Su-an,*

> *To Nurŭngji in Hwangju,*
> *To Yangadong in Pongsan,*
> *To Ssukumul in Chaeryŏng,*
> *To Tokgut in Haeju:*
> *Let's go, if you wish to go.*[5]

(Then she speaks in a traditional narrative mode.)

> *In a big town, put a tile roof on your house;*
> *Let's reap grain in every season and*
> *Bear babies every month, twelve times a year.*

WIFE: Are you saying you'll give birth to twelve babies a year?

CH'U-WOL: When there's a leap month, I can have thirteen babies a year.[6]

WIFE: You greedy bitch! You can't have all of them!
  (The WIFE runs headlong into CH'U-WOL, striking her with her forehead. But it is the WIFE who falls backwards hurt; CH'U-WOL is perfectly fine.)

YI CHI: Sister!

CH'U-WOL: *(Runs out.)* Doctor! Doctor!

TŎK-JUNG: Blind man, blind man!

FATHER: *(Entering the stage.)* Who's calling me?

TŎK-JUNG: Here! Over here!

FATHER: What's the patient's family name?

YI CHI: It's Shim. Her name is Shim Tal-lae.

FATHER: *(Feeling her pulse with his fingers.)* She smells awful. What a terrible odor! Her body is rotten halfway through. I'll have to charge you a lot.

TŎK-JUNG: How much?

FATHER: A hundred bucks.

YI CHI: One and eight bits. Can't you make it any cheaper than that?

FATHER: Go, fetch bearers. I'll have her taken away in a coffin.

TŎK-JUNG: You mean, she finally "cut a cold fart"?

FATHER: She has passed away.

TŎK-JUNG: That's good! Bearers! Pallbearers!

YI CHI: What about mourners to follow the coffin?

FATHER: You mean she has no mourners?

YI CHI: Ch'un-p'ung's in prison for embezzling government money. Tal-lae came here to save him by taking this government post. Now that she's dead, I don't know what to do.

FATHER: We can't take a coffin away without a mourner.

WIFE: (*Suddenly getting up, ecstatically.*) Look here!

YI CHI: Yes, sister. I'm here.

WIFE: Was it Ch'u-wol who hit me, who cut my life short?

TŎK-JUNG: Hey, be honest. You hit her first.

WIFE: That bitch sang so nice. Let me tell you something—I'd go to Pukmang Mountain gladly if I could just hear her sing one more time.

YI CHI: But she's not here. She's already gone.

WIFE: Then I'll go to Pukmang Mountain if I can wear her dress— even just once.[7]

TŎK-JUNG: I'll fetch it. (*Runs out. The* WIFE *lies back down on the ground.*)

FATHER: Look here, this corpse is going back and forth from life to death like a fish jumping in and out of the water. Before the earth god gets angry and strikes us down for this travesty, we should call in a shaman for an exorcism.

YI CHI: Where can we find a shaman?

FATHER: He's here.

YI CHI: Where?

FATHER: Right here. *Moi.*

YI CHI: Take the money. (*Counting out money.*) One bit, eight bits. (*Abruptly bumps his head against the* FATHER. *The* FATHER *runs away clutching his face.*) I'll be the shaman. Now listen. (*Sings a mournful tune.*)

> Over there—
> Is the field untilled
> because there was no plow?
> Or is it fallow
> because there was no plowman?

(*Pallbearers enter, responding to* YI CHI's *song during the following refrain. They carry the* WIFE *on their shoulders as if her body were in a coffin.*)

CHORUS OF PALLBEARERS: Ah, ha, ha, hei, hei, yo.

YI CHI: *Plant wheat in a rich field,*

Grow rye in a poor one.

Plant beans along the side.

CHORUS OF PALLBEARERS: Ah, ha, ha, hei, hei, yo!

(TŎK-JUNG *and* CH'UN-P'UNG *enter.* TŎK-JUNG *carries* CH'U-WOL's *dress and covers the* WIFE's *body with it.* CH'UN-P'UNG *wails in a singing mode.*)

CH'UN-P'UNG: *Aigoo!* You and I shared a fate arranged in a previous existence and made a promise to each other for this life. Have you forgotten it already? How could you leave me? My poor, pitiful darling, my Ch'u-wol! Your soul flown already? Ah me, your poor body, lying there speechless.

YI CHI: What's going on here? Who are you moaning for? What do you mean, "Ch'u-wol"?

TŎK-JUNG: When he saw the dress, he asked what was wrong with Ch'u-wol. I hated him for caring for her so much, so I said she'd croaked. That's why he's howling.

YI CHI: Look, you've got the wrong body.

CH'UN-P'UNG: *(Wails.)* Aigoo, aigoo———

TŎK-JUNG: What does it matter? Anyway, we need wailing so we can go on with the funeral procession. I don't care if it's for Ch'u-wol or Chew-dick.

CH'UN-P'UNG: *Aigoo, aigoo*———

TŎK-JUNG: Go on. Keep on bawling. It doesn't matter *who* you're crying for. It's perfect. In fact, it's just the kind of wailing we need to carry out the coffin. *(Joining* CH'UN-P'UNG, *bawls.)* Whaaa———, whaaa———

WIFE: *(From underneath the dress.)* Hey! What's all this racket about?

YI CHI: A shaman's feeding ghosts on the street to exorcise evil spirits.

WIFE: A plague on that son of a bitch! Who does he think he is, "*aigooing*" in the middle of a holy ritual. All that "*aigooing*" woke me up from a good, sound sleep. Let me look at that bastard's filthy mug. *(She raises her body over the heads of the* PALLBEARERS.)

TŎK-JUNG: Sister! You're not dead yet?

CH'UN-P'UNG: Ch'u-wol–ah!

YI CHI: Her face is a little uglier, but she's certainly Ch'u-wol.

TŎK-JUNG: Oh, oh! You're pulling my leg.

CH'UN-P'UNG: Don't argue with each other when you see a person coming back from the dead. At a time like this, you should pray, not pick a fight. *(Making a formal bow.)* This is my prayer to the King of the Underworld, my prayer, my solemn prayer. *(Keeps bowing.)*

WIFE: *(Beaming with joy.)* Is anybody there?

YI CHI: Yes, I'm here.

WIFE: Should I be happy or mad? Should I talk to him respectfully or just be free and easy?

YI CHI: You can be polite to your husband and casual with us. Just act like you did when you were alive.

WIFE: I'm not sure if it will work out in the end. What happens when he finds out I'm not his little Ch'u-wol?

TŎK-JUNG: Don't worry about it. Who cares if you're Ch'u-wol or Chew-dick? What matters is that you'll be with your husband now. Don't worry about it and relax. Just think that you'll have one more chance to live with your husband—all because of two brilliant people like Yi Chi and me. Don't you know that good people like us are hard to find these days?

WIFE: What a crock! You guys are such a joke. Are you saying that I should be happy? Happy to be with my husband?

TŎK-JUNG: Why are you yelling?

WIFE: Maybe I should laugh, then?

TŎK-JUNG: I quit. You're acting like a snotty child.

WIFE: Where are you going?

TŎK-JUNG: None of your fucking business. Wherever I want to go.

WIFE: Whaaa! I can't take it anymore. Do you think I'm all right? You think my body is still okay? It feels like my blood's flowing backwards, my hands and feet are all twisted, and my bowels are rotten to the core. I can't feel the ground when I walk, I can't even tell which direction is which when I look around. You jerk!

Are you being mean because you think I look like I'm alive? How can an insignificant animal like you dare to talk to me like this. What's a husband anyway? Why should I be so humiliated because of a husband? I don't care. Go, if you want to. I'm done with the whole thing, too. I don't give a damn about my husband any more. Boy! That feels good. It feels like flying away. I'll fly away, fly away. I'm going back. Yee-ha! *(While clapping and singing, she dances.)*

CH'UN-P'UNG: *(Joining the* WIFE'S *song.)*

> Mountain, mountain, Okmae Mountain,
> You become Flood Mountain when it rains.

(They dance so wildly and energetically that the stage soon looks like a dance floor.)

TŎK-JUNG'S VOICE: Sister, what happened to the limp in your left leg? *(The* WIFE *performs a "humpback's dance.")*[8]

TŎK-JUNG'S VOICE: What did you do with the three little wart brothers on your left hand?

WIFE: One died hit by a pinecone, another was cut by eels, the last one fell off by itself after having a stroke.

TŎK-JUNG'S VOICE: Sister, why do you wear a broken copper chopstick in your hair? Did you lose your gold and silver hairpins?

WIFE: I sold my silver and gold hairpins at a pawnshop to pay for my trip to the Underworld. Shweee——. *(Stops dancing.)* Look, husband dear, it's been a long time.

CH'UN-P'UNG: What happened to your face? You used to look pretty and cute. Why's your face all rough and twisted, out of shape, ugly?

WIFE: Stop saying that. Dear husband, we're blessed because we finally meet each other again after such a long time. It's time to celebrate. Why don't we just have a good time together? *(Singing.)* Happy to see you. So good to see you . . .

(They start dancing together in a seductive manner. With her body clinging to CH'UN-P'UNG'S, *the* WIFE *makes overt sexual advances to him.* CH'UN-

P'UNG *falls down on his back and the* WIFE *crawls over* CH'UN-P'UNG'S *head.)*

WIFE: *(In the pain of childbirth.)* Aigoo! It hurts! Help!

YI CHI: Here I am.

WIFE: Please hold my hand. I think I'm gonna pass out.

TŎK-JUNG: *(Holding her hands.)* What's wrong with you? You just had your very last baby and gave it away. If you can't bear any more babies, why are you being so indecent on the street? I'm ashamed of you.

WIFE: Look, at age seventy I've just had sex with a man. That's something to celebrate. Why do you say you're ashamed? *(Looking back at* CH'UN-P'UNG, *who is squirming on the ground.)* My god! How big he is! *(Passes out.)*

YI CHI: Sister!

TŎK-JUNG: You know, I thought she was rushing things a bit. Maybe indigestion.

WIFE: *(Painfully.)* I'm glad that I bore a son. *(Dies.)*

YI CHI: Oh, no! Sister!

TŎK-JUNG: She gave birth to her own husband—like he was her son. Golly, now that's being greedy. No wonder she passed away.

CH'UN-P'UNG: *(Looking at his* WIFE, *lying dead.)* Is she dead? Aigoo, Ch'u-wol has really passed away. She's too young to die so suddenly. Medicine, bring some medicine! *P'aedok* roots for cold, *Weryŏng* herbs for diarrhea, *Soch'e* roots for gout, *Yuksin* leaves for constipation . . . Please open your eyes! My poor, miserable Ch'u-wol! You died without taking any of these medicines. *(Wails.)*

YI CHI: I know it's a great sorrow that she died. But what's done is done. Let's offer a ritual to comfort her spirit so that she can make an easy journey to paradise.

(CH'U-WOL enters, bringing small bells and a fan, and performs a ritual.)

CH'U-WOL: *(Her spirit having entered a shaman's body, she sings a shaman's recitation, calling on the spirit of the dead; then, in a narrative mode, speaks.)* I came back, I came back. I came borrowing the shaman's mouth and her body. I couldn't accomplish what I set out to do in this world. And here I am, a traveler from the Underworld. (*Cries as a shaman.*) Place your spirit in the bowl for spirits, carry your soul on the platter for souls, and make a safe journey to paradise.

(*She rings the small bells, and everyone joins her dance and exits while dancing.*)

YI CHI: May you go to a good place, as everyone wishes.

TŎK-JUNG: Yi Chi, we're all alone. Let's be on our way, too.

YI CHI: By the way, why did we come up here?

TŎK-JUNG: To get some wild ginsaeng.

YI CHI: That's not it.

TŎK-JUNG: Did we come here for bellflower roots?

YI CHI: I don't think so.

TŎK-JUNG: Oh, no, Yi Chi! I think I forgot!

YI CHI: What, what are we going to do for my eighty-year-old mother, then? You know, you should just go and die. Why should you live?

(TŎK-JUNG *hits his forehead against the ground and falls backwards.*)

YI CHI: Oh, no! Hey, Tŏk-jung! I didn't mean it. What a temper you have! I spoke harshly, but it was out of . . . affection. Hello! Anybody, out there? My young brother has suddenly taken sick. Fetch a doctor for him, please! (*Pause.*) Doctor, doctor! (*There is no sound.*)

NOTES

1. *Yŏngsanp'o,* located in North Korea, is the legendary place where the Dragon King of the East Sea and his seven sons came to the aid of the forty-ninth king of Silla. Tŏk-jung and Yi Chi have likewise come to this site to do good works.

2. *Pyongyang* is now the capital of North Korea.

3. *Kicked the bucket* is a free translation of a Korean idiom for dying, literally, "put down my spoon."

4. *Kok-ye.* A reference to one of many Confucian texts on correct conduct.

The Wife searches for her husband.

5. *Let's go, if you wish to go* is a folk song consisting almost entirely of the names of famous places to visit in various cities and towns.

6. *Leap month.* Into the Korean lunar calendar, a leap month, or intercalary month, was sometimes introduced.

7. *Pukmang Mountain* is a legendary mountain where the dead reside.

8. *A humpback's dance* mimics and exaggerates the movements of people who are handicapped with this affliction.

A shamanist ritual to appease death.

LIFECORD

Cast of Characters

THE SA YUK SIN, *six scholars who died in 1456 attempting to restore Tanjong to the throne, which had been usurped by his uncle, Sejo:*

SŎNG SAM-MUN

PAK P'AENG-NYŎN

YU SŎNG-WON

YU ŬNG-BO

YI KAE

HA WI-JI

TANJONG, *formerly the king*

KING SEJO, *uncle to Tanjong and formerly Prince Su-yang*

SHIN SUK-JU, *a courtier at the court of Sejo*

PAK CHUNG-LIM, *Pak P'aeng-nyŏn's father*

LADY PAK SUN-ŎN, *Pak P'aeng-nyŏn's daughter-in-law*

SERVANT *of Lady Pak*

WIFE *of Servant*

WANG PANG-YŎN, *chief prosecutor*

ACT ONE

THE COURT

(King TANJONG'*s announcement of his abdication of the crown is heard.)*
VOICE OF TANJONG: My uncle is blessed with great virtues, and his

contributions to the kingdom are as great as those of the revered Zhou Gong of China. I am still young, as was King Cheng, and the situation I now face is as difficult as that which he once confronted. Even as King Cheng sought the help of his uncle, Zhou Gong, I ask the same of my uncle. Assist me as Zhou Gong helped King Cheng.[1]

(The SA YUK SIN *cry out in unison.)*

SA YUK SIN: Your majesty, you should not do this!

VOICE: *(Sings the following poem by Pak P'aeng-nyŏn.)*

> *Crows are black[2]*
> *Even when covered by snow,*
> *The full and splendid moon*
> *Shines all the brighter*
> *In the dark,*
> *Devoted to Him alone,*
> *My heart will never change.*

(Among the SA YUK SIN, YU-SŎNG WON *plunges a dagger into his chest and falls down.)*

SEJO'S ACCUSATION

SEJO: Sŏng Sam-mun, why do you betray me?

SŎNG SAM-MUN: No one will call it betrayal. I merely restored the rightful king to the throne. Everyone in this kingdom knows my position. Each of us has his own master to serve. One cannot serve two kings; it is as unnatural as two suns in the sky.

SEJO: But you have been serving me all this while. Why did you wait until now? Why didn't you try to stop me before I ascended the throne?

SŎNG SAM-MUN: Back then, I knew that I could not resist the powerful tide. I had to wait for the right moment.

SEJO: But you have already received a fiefdom from me, and now you are breaking your faith. You are a worthless traitor!

SŎNG SAM-MUN: My lord, I never received a fiefdom from you. The land belongs to my king—Tanjong—and he is still alive. How can I be your subject, then? (*A torturer presses a hot iron into* SŎNG SAM-MUN's *leg and smoke rises from his burning thigh. He screams.*) My lord, your torture is indeed painful. (SŎNG SAM-MUN *recognizes the courtier* SHIN SUK-JU *and addresses him.*) You betrayer! How is it possible that you forgot your promise to Great King Sejong? When we were admitted into the Academy, the Great King asked you and me to take care of his grandson after he was gone.[3] He was holding Tanjong in his arms, strolling in the garden. I can still hear his generous voice. How can you forget that? I did not realize who you were then! You are an evil bastard!

(*Smoke rises from his thigh. He screams and falls.*)

SEJO: (*To* PAK P'AENG-NYŎN.) I shall forgive you if you vow to serve me.

PAK P'AENG-NYŎN: Serve you? When did I become your subject?

(*Smoke rises from his thigh. He falls with a scream.*)

SEJO: (*To the scholar* YI KAE.) All of you are my old friends. How can you bring this upon me? If you only say that you were not involved in this crime, I will not punish you.

YI KAE: (*Laughs.*) You have charged me with the crime of high treason. Finish me off, then. What more do you want from me?

(*Smoke rises. Screams. All six scholars collapse on the ground.*)

VOICE: (*Singing.*)

> *When the hot irons press, listen to them scream.*
> *How wrong to serve Prince Su-yang, not our rightful king.*
> *Do they give up life so readily because life is meaningless?*
> *Probably not. Dying thus is an honorable luxury.*

PAK CHUNG-LIM'S HOUSE

(*Prostrate in front of the family shrine,* PAK CHUNG-LIM, *father of Pak P'aeng-nyŏn, speaks to the ancestral altar.*)

PAK CHUNG-LIM: Dearest ancestors, I kneel and pray to you as our family line is coming to an end. I am deeply ashamed of myself.

How shall I face you in the underworld? They will kill all of my family—parents, children, even newborn babes. It is clear that our family line will be extinguished. I am to blame. Oh, dear ancestors!

(In the midst of PAK*'s prayer, the* SERVANT *enters, carrying his newborn son wrapped in a blanket. His* WIFE *follows, her arms extended straight out from her body and tied to a bar that crosses behind her shoulders. As the* SERVANT *places the baby on the ground, his* WIFE *frantically attempts to pick it up, finally even with her mouth, but in vain.)*

SERVANT: Master!

PAK CHUNG-LIM: Has someone come from the palace? I will go soon.

SERVANT: Master!

PAK CHUNG-LIM: Who are you?

SERVANT: I am the servant of Pak Sun, your second grandson. This is my wife. My Lady is expecting a child soon.

PAK CHUNG-LIM: *(Hangs his head in despair.)* The more to be pitied! The child will be born only to be killed. Or they will kill the mother even while she carries the child. What an unhappy fate she will have to bear as a young mother! Ancestors, I pray that you stop wreaking this destruction on our family.

SERVANT: *(Unwrapping the blanket.)* This is my son, born only two days ago. My wife and I have already talked to each other about a certain idea. If My Lady bears a son, let us switch the babies so that Your Lordship can preserve your family line . . . although we may be presumptuous to suggest such a notion to you.

PAK CHUNG-LIM: What are you talking about now?

SERVANT: If My Lady . . . *(Shakes with tears.)* If My Lady bears a son, exchange the babies . . . so that your Lordship's family can continue . . .

PAK CHUNG-LIM: Give him to me. *(Kneels down in front of the family shrine while holding the baby in his arms.)* Ancestors, have mercy on us. And protect this pitiful one's life as he goes on his way. He shall die so that our family, the Pak family of Sun-ch'ŏn, may live. May this sacrifice not be in vain.

(*The* WIFE *faints to the ground, crying for her baby.*)

WIFE: My heart, my Ch'ang-ji-ya![4]

THE EXECUTION GROUND

SHIN SUK-JU: Destroy the whole family of the traitor, Sŏng Sam-mun: his father, Sŏng Sŭng; his brothers, Sŏng Sam-bing, Sŏng Sam-go, Sŏng Sam-sŏng; his sons, Sŏng Maeng-ch'ŏl, Sŏng Maeng-p'yŏng, Sŏng Maeng-jong; his grandsons, Sŏng hyŏn, Sŏng T'aek; and so on. Execute them all!

(*Court music is played for a moment.*)

Kill the whole family of the traitor, Pak P'aeng-nyŏn: his father, Pak Chung-lim; his younger brothers, Pak Ki-nyŏn, Pak In-nyŏn, Pak Tae-nyŏn, Pak Yŏng-nyŏn; his sons, Pak Hŏn, Pak Sun, Pak Pun; and his grandsons. Execute them all!

(*Court music is played for a moment.*)

Exterminate the whole family of the traitor, Yi Kae: his younger brother, Yi Yun-gi; his son, Yi Kong-hŭi, and so on. Execute them all!

(*Court music is played for a moment.*)

Execute the whole family of the traitor, Yu Sŏng-won; his sons, Yu Ki-ryŏn, Yu Song-ryŏn, and so on. Execute them all!

(*Court music is played for a moment, then a short song accompanied by instrumental court music is heard.*)

VOICE: (*Singing a poem by Wang Pang-yŏn.*)

> *I walk into the deep, snowbound forest;*[5]
> *In early summer, one cannot see beneath the ice,*
> *But water is flowing underneath all the same.*
> *Whatever is said of me,*
> *You will fathom my heart, my beloved!*

Sejo's Court

*(A commotion suggestive of a fight is heard in the distance. We see King
SEJO, apparently confronting the ghosts of his executed subjects. SEJO's actions
suggest that the ghosts are floating in the air.)*

SEJO: You impertinent spirits! What do you want? How dare you
befoul this court of sacred order! *(A woman's scream is heard.)* What
is that? Who dares to bring a woman here?

VOICE: She is the wife of Pak P'aeng-nyŏn's son. She is expecting a
baby.

PAK CHUNG-LIM'S VOICE: No, let go of me. Let go of me. Finish me off,
you devils! *(Runs onto the stage, followed by his grandson's wife.)*

SEJO: Who are you? What . . . how did you get in here?

PAK CHUNG-LIM: Don't worry. I will soon go to the execution
ground. But before I go, I wish to ask you a favor. *(Indicating the
woman.)* This is my grandson's wife, who is carrying his child.
They were about to kill her because of the baby inside her, so I
brought her here to plead for her life.

SEJO: Don't you know that no one can rescind the order of the
king?

PAK CHUNG-LIM: I have faith in you. I brought her here to beg for
her life. You would not sacrifice a pregnant woman by throwing
her into the middle of the ocean, unless, of course, you are a
brutal sailor.

SEJO: Are you referring to what happened on my way to Japan as
ambassador?

PAK CHUNG-LIM: My son, P'aeng-nyŏn, told me that you once saved
a pregnant woman's life from murderous sailors.[6] You told them
it was wrong to sacrifice a woman to save their lives. My son
gained great admiration for you from that deed and never
stopped praising you as a man of virtue, generosity, and breadth
of mind.

SEJO: You mock me.

PAK CHUNG-LIM: I am only asking you to save her life.

SEJO: But this case is different.

PAK CHUNG-LIM: Now that you have stolen the crown from your nephew, you have changed indeed. I will kill you before I die. *(Drawing his sword.)* Today I regret that I stopped Sŏng Sŭng, father of Sŏng Sam-mun, from killing you.

(He lunges at SEJO. At the same time, the ghosts of the six scholars rush out onto the stage. Momentarily confused, Pak hesitates. LADY SUN-ŎN takes out her dagger and plunges it into the back of her grandfather-in-law. He collapses.)

LADY PAK: My Lord, I swear by the blood on my hands that as soon as my baby is born, I will kill it just as I have done here. But please let me give birth to my child.

SEJO: You killed your grandfather! For such a crime, you cannot escape the penalty of death. And yet you dare ask not only for your life but for the chance to give birth to your baby? What gall you have!

LADY PAK: If you let me deliver my child, Your Majesty will have one more life to kill.

SEJO: I take no pleasure in executing the members of your family.

LADY PAK: It is a fault in me that I am expecting a child during such a crisis. It is my responsibility to take its life. Please let me kill the child with my own hands, I beg you . . . I will never let you touch my baby! Only over my own dead body, never!
(Pause.)

SEJO: Before my eyes, you have just murdered your husband's grandfather. Now you are begging to kill your own baby. How pitiful your life is!

LADY PAK: How pitiful *you* are to steal the throne and kill the families of your subjects! People will pity your fateful life as much as mine.

SEJO: You speak like a man. I would have consulted you on political matters if you were a man.

LADY PAK: If you had, you would never have robbed Tanjong of his throne.
(Long silence.)

SEJO: They say that an expert archer like Ch'ŏn-kyun never shot a helpless mouse. I want you to bring your child into this world. Such a child is not the offspring of a traitor but of a loyal subject. Go away, then! If it is a boy, kill him and bring him to me; but if it is girl, you may live together. *(Exits.)*

LADY PAK: I thank the king for his kindness. *(Embracing* PAK CHUNG-LIM's *body violently, cries out.)* Oh, Grandfather!

VOICE: *(Singing.)*

> *She collapses to the ground*
> *And cries in sorrow:*
> Aigoo, *the grandfather dies.*
> *He has finally gone.*
> *What shall I do?*

LADY PAK: *(Speaking to her dead grandfather.)* You shall have a great-grandson. It was your plan. He will carry on our family line. *(The Six Scholars move together as if in a ritual.)*

LADY PAK: I pray to you.

SA YUK SIN: I pray to you.

LADY PAK: To the great mountains of the country.

SA YUK SIN: To the great mountains of the country.

LADY PAK: To the great temples of the many Buddhas.

SA YUK SIN: To the great temples of the many Buddhas.

LADY PAK: To the fifty-three Buddhas.

SA YUK SIN: To the fifty-three Buddhas.

LADY PAK: To the five hundred disciples of the Buddha and to the Merciful Buddha.

SA YUK SIN: To the five hundred disciples of the Buddha and to the Merciful Buddha.

LADY PAK: I pray to the God of the Four Directions and the seven stars of the Great Bear.

SA YUK SIN: I pray to the God of the Four Directions and the seven stars of the Great Bear.

LADY PAK: The Pak family line of the Sun-ch'ŏn clan has been carried on through Pak Chung-lim, he of the hall of accomplished scholarship, and Pak P'aeng-nyŏn of the hall of shining wisdom.

The family line is now in my hands. Please, have mercy on me and grant my wish. Please . . .

SA YUK SIN: Please . . .

(She and the Six Scholars perform a ceremonial dance representing childbirth. The SERVANT *enters carrying his child and exchanges him with the newborn infant.* LADY PAK *stabs the* SERVANT*'s child with a dagger and then kills herself.)*

ACT TWO

THE COURT

(Enter SEJO *and* SHIN SUK-JU.*)*

SEJO: *(Shouts).* Did I not condemn him to exile? Yŏngwol is far away, hundreds of miles from here. Leave him alone.

SHIN SUK-JU: *(Shouts back.)* But what if someone communicates secretly with him in Yŏngwol? Should you leave him alone then?

SEJO: Who would dare go to Yŏngwol? Everyone knows that it would mean the destruction of his whole family.

SHIN SUK-JU: I could go myself.

SEJO: I order you not to.

SHIN SUK-JU: Leave me alone.

SEJO: Then you leave Tanjong alone. Sŏng Sam-mun and Pak P'aeng-nyŏn should have left him alone. Tanjong trusts me. Leave him alone so that he can live in peace. I will kill anyone who tries to take advantage of that innocent boy. And this applies to you too, my good sir.

(Pause.)

SHIN SUK-JU: There are many kinds of men in the court. Some are foolish, some are greedy, but all of them are your subjects.

SEJO: Even if Tanjong should die, fools will remain fools, and the greedy will still be greedy. Let us assume that Tanjong's death would actually make fools smart and the greedy generous. Then what? Would his death still be worthwhile? Why do you urge me to kill my own blood?

SHIN SUK-JU: But there are too many fools hovering about in court.

SEJO: Time will change that. Just wait a while.

SHIN SUK-JU: That little "while" could be long enough to cause you harm.

SEJO: Leave Tanjong alone, I say! *(Touches* SHIN SUK-JU *on his shoulder. Pause.)* I cherish our friendship. I befriended you because I knew you were open-minded and clever. You are also wise and not petty about trivial matters. Without your advice and devotion, I would not be king today. But you baffle me now. Why are you asking me to commit such an inconceivable crime? My dear friend, do not squander my admiration for you.

SHIN SUK-JU: I do not deserve Your Majesty's kind words. I am simply worried that many of your subjects may turn traitor if you permit Tanjong to survive. Their attempts to restore Tanjong will undermine your government and the kingdom. And, at any rate, how many courtiers can you send to the execution field? I wish only to stop more killing. Please extend your royal favor and save these living souls. Make them your servants. I tremble to say it to you, but I ask that you make Tanjong king of the dead, not the living.

SEJO: *(Shaking his head.)* Tanjong is as good as dead if you leave him alone.

SHIN SUK-JU: I only mean . . .

SEJO: I warn you, my friend. Do not say another word about Tanjong to me. Otherwise . . .

(Suddenly, the six ghosts appear and surround SEJO. *They hold a bloodstained baby's blanket.)*

SEJO: Go away . . .

SHIN SUK-JU: What are you so frightened of?

SEJO: Don't you see them? . . . They come to me everyday with this bloody blanket . . . *(The six ghosts spread the baby's bedding over* SEJO's *hand.)* Take it away . . . Please . . . take it away!

SHIN SUK-JU: What are you holding?

SEJO: Take it away!

SHIN SUK-JU: *(Picking up the blanket.)* Isn't this the blan———... the blanket that wrapped the body of Pak P'aeng-nyŏn's grandson? Why are you carrying it?

SEJO: Didn't you see these men give it to me just now? . . . Why would I carry such a horrible thing?

SHIN SUK-JU: What are you saying? Who gave you what?

(The six ghosts leave, beckoning SEJO to follow.)

SEJO: *(Following after them.)* Wait . . . stay there.

SHIN SUK-JU: Your Majesty! Where are you going? *(Shaking his head, SEJO exits.)* Oh, who can be sure that Tanjong is so naive and innocent? Sitting out there in Yŏngwol, hundreds of miles away, he is driving My Lord mad, even as he does the subjects of the king.

YŏNGWOL, KANGWON PROVINCE

(The chief prosecutor, WANG PANG-YŎN, gives TANJONG a bowl of poison. TANJONG bows twice in the direction of King SEJO's court, drinks the poison, and falls down dead.)

VOICE: *(Sings another song by Wang Pang-yŏn).*

> Lost in the dark,
> I cried all the way,
> Not knowing where to go,
> Leaving my dead lover behind,
> Far, far away.

(TANJONG's body is dragged out by the feet.)

THE PALACE

VOICE: Chief prosecutor, Wang Pang-yŏn!

(WANG PANG-YŎN enters. SHIN SUK-JU follows, carrying a white "umbilical jar.")[7]

SHIN SUK-JU: I commend you for your work, handling affairs at Yŏngwol so admirably. How is the former king, Tanjong?

WANG PANG-YŎN: He is in good health.

SHIN SUK-JU: I hear Yŏngwol is a very beautiful place.

WANG PANG-YŎN: He never goes out, so he cannot enjoy the scenery.

SHIN SUK-JU: Three times today the king asked me if you had arrived. When you meet him, please give him a detailed report. I have awaited your arrival as eagerly as His Majesty. *(Pause.)* I understand that the day you left for Yŏngwol with Tanjong, many people gathered wanting to restore him to the throne. Some of them even dug up this jar from the ground, filled with the umbilical cords of the royal forebears, and intended to present it to Tanjong with your aid.

WANG PANG-YŎN: I am so old and incompetent that all I can do is attend Tanjong. I cannot think of anything else.

SHIN SUK-JU: *(Unrolls a large scroll of white cloth on which the names of the alleged conspirators are listed.)* Do you recognize any of the names written here?

WANG PANG-YŎN: These are members of the court, are they not?

SHIN SUK-JU: If you add your son, grandson, and all of your relatives to this list, how many more heads will there be? *(Pause.)* When the king comes, repeat what I just said.

WANG PANG-YŎN: What do you mean?

SHIN SUK-JU: Just say, "While I was in Yŏngwol, there were certain people who communicated secretly with Tanjong." Then read the list of names of those involved.

WANG PANG-YŎN: I must repeat that I never . . .

SHIN SUK-JU: *(Shouts).* Hundreds of people have died because of this fifteen-year-old boy. Six loyal subjects of the king were put to death. In the house of Pak P'aeng-nyŏn, even a child fresh from the womb was killed by his own mother. Look here! *(Hurls the swaddling cloth at* WANG PANG-YŎN.*)* How many more people must be sacrificed because of one child? A woman slays her son with her own hands, simply because he happens to have been born a great-grandson to a traitor. No! I will not allow any more blood-shed . . . We have already killed six loyal subjects. That is enough.

WANG PANG-YŎN: But Tanjong . . .

SHIN SUK-JU: You will not be harmed. Neither will the other courtiers. But if you do not tell the king what I told you to say, all shall be executed, including you. If you do as I say *(Pause)*, Tanjong will be given the penalty of death. But the king needs evidence. And it must be you who provides it.

WANG PANG-YŎN: *(Beating the ground.)* But this is terrible! What horrible thing have I . . .

SHIN SUK-JU: What do you mean? Has something happened?

WANG PANG-YŎN: *(Shaking his head as if crying.)* While I was in Yŏngwol, I secretly contacted the followers of Tanjong. But I was worried that our conspiracy would be revealed to the king. *(Breaks down and cries.)* I was so frightened that I couldn't sleep . . . Day and night, a rainy wind blew. I couldn't sleep at all . . . I was at my wit's end.

SHIN SUK-JU: And then?

WANG PANG-YŎN: When I was escorting Tanjong to Yŏngwol, my mother passed away. I couldn't go home. Instead, I wrote her epitaph. It broke my heart that I couldn't present her a memorial offering.

SHIN SUK-JU: *(Shouts.)* What are you saying? *(Grabbing the collar of* WANG PANG-YŎN'*s shirt).* What happened in Yŏngwol? Is Tanjong all right?

*(*WANG PANG-YŎN *shakes his head.)*

SHIN SUK-JU: How is he? Tell me right now!

WANG PANG-YŎN: I executed him . . . poisoned him in the king's name.

(Long silence.)

SHIN SUK-JU: Even though you are a loyal subject of the king in every respect, you nevertheless cannot be pardoned for killing the former king without His Majesty's order. *(Draws out a dagger and stabs* WANG PANG-YŎN. WANG PANG-YŎN *collapses on the ground.)*

Your Majesty! *(Prostrate, crying.)* Where is His Majesty? My Lord! Tanjong is dead! Your Majesty, in your own name pronounce that you have destroyed the abdicated king at last. *(Stands up.)* Let me go to Yŏngwol myself. I shall fetch his body before this bloodshed breeds rebellion.

SEJO'S COURT

(The SERVANT *and his* WIFE *enter. Her hair is disheveled and she murmurs wildly to herself, clearly having lost her mind. Her husband carries a baby, his former master's son. He gently offers the baby to her for feeding, but she pushes the baby away, even though her breasts are swollen with milk. He pushes the baby to her breast, but she refuses. After several attempts, he rolls up his shirt and attempts to nurse the baby himself. The* WIFE *roars with laughter, then abruptly stops and weeps for her own child.)*

WIFE: Oh, my Ch'ang-ji! Bring my baby back. Ch'ang-ji-ya!

(Enter SEJO.*)*

SEJO: What is all this commotion? *(*WIFE *runs away, letting out a sharp cry like a frightened deer.)* What is this? What are you mumbling? Come closer. *(The six ghosts surround him, closing in on him like shadows.)* Lift your face. Who . . . what are you, and where do you come from? If you are not a ghost, you must know I am king. How impertinent you are. I told you to go away. How dare you linger before me!

SA YUK SIN: Send a messenger to Yŏngwol, or you will be in grave danger.

SEJO: Yŏngwol? Do you mean something has happened to Tanjong?

SA YUK SIN: Treason.

SEJO: Who . . . ?

SA YUK SIN: Shin Suk-ju, he of the hall of rare wisdom, has conspired. *(Pause.)*

SEJO: Treason means assassinating a king. But I am safe and sound here. What is more, Shin Suk-ju is my attendant.

SA YUK SIN: Shin Suk-ju has left for Yŏngwol.

SEJO: To what purpose?

SA YUK SIN: He killed the former king.

SEJO: *(Shouts.)* He is innocent! You scoundrels! Whom are you trying to slander? We have been friends since we accompanied the Chinese envoys during the reign of the Great King. We have shared our fate together. To disgrace him is to disgrace me.

SA YUK SIN: Shin Suk-ju is a traitor. He betrayed the Great King Sejong.

SEJO: He has been loyal to me.

SA YUK SIN: But now he has betrayed you as well.

SEJO: I thought you resembled the six dead scholars. Everything you say crosses me. I will cut off your heads outside the palace. *(The six ghosts point at* WANG PANG-YŎN.*)*

SA YUK SIN: Wang Pang-yŏn, the chief prosecutor . . .

SEJO: Who?

SA YUK SIN: Shin Suk-ju of the hall of rare wisdom . . .

SEJO: The old proverb says, "Happy faces make one glad; gloomy faces make one sad." Now they show me dead faces. They must be telling me I am surrounded by death. *(Yells.)* Hurry, send a messenger to Shin Suk-ju. What is the matter with him? I have always thought of him as my own flesh and blood. Did he kill the pitiful boy at last? Has he turned against me? *(Lifts up his head.)* I will cut off my flesh and blood. Go to Yŏngwol and behead them both. No, I will kill them myself. *(He runs out.)*

AN OPEN FIELD

VOICE: Hush! Kneel down. Here come the funeral flags.

(The six ghosts enter with funeral flags inscribed with the names and ranks of the dead.)

SEJO: Where is this funeral bier going? Who is the chief mourner?

SHIN SUK-JU: *(Prostrates himself.)* My Lord, you are the chief mourner.

SEJO: I? You ignorant fool, you killed that child! *(He pulls out his sword.)* Prepare to die!

(The SA YUK SIN *intercept him with the funeral flags.)*

SA YUK SIN: My Lord, take care. You are in mourning.

SEJO: *(Dropping his sword, he yells while tearing the flags into pieces.)* Take the funeral bier away. Tanjong is not dead!

SHIN SUK-JU: Your Royal Highness. It is done. Don't shed any more blood over this matter.

SEJO: No blood has been spilled. Tanjong has not died.

SHIN SUK-JU: Please give the royal order. It is not too late. Waste no more time. Announce that you have administered poison to Tanjong. Then he will die by your order, Your Majesty.

SEJO: Announce that I am dead.

SHIN SUK-JU: Do not let Tanjong die in vain.

SEJO: *(Lamenting.)* What sorrow, what sorrow! I killed him in the end . . . How can I ever join the line of my ancestors? I cannot face them now. Perhaps I shall not even be able to die. *(Yells.)* No, I will not let him die. I will revive him.

SHIN SUK-JU: Control yourself, Your Majesty!

(The funeral flags start moving.)

SEJO: Return Tanjong to me.

SHIN SUK-JU: Please do not abandon your people.

SA YUK SIN: My Lord!

SEJO: Who are you to call me lord?

SA YUK SIN: We are the ones who shall die soon.

SEJO: Why are you here?

SA YUK SIN: We communicated with Tanjong secretly.

SEJO: I am as glad to see you as to see Tanjong himself. You shall help me.

SA YUK SIN: Leave the former king to us and issue a royal order.

SHIN SUK-JU: My Lord!

SA YUK SIN: Your Majesty!

(The monotonous sound of a bell is heard.)

SHIN SUK-JU: A royal command is about to be pronounced!

SA YUK SIN: The royal command!

(Long silence.)

SEJO: I executed him. Send the Sa Yuk-Sin along to the other world with him.

(Funeral flags, waving in the air, are carried off the stage. The SERVANT *steps out, holding a baby wrapped in a blanket.)*

SERVANT: My master. O my Lord!

SEJO: Who is this?

SERVANT: Punish me. I deserve the severest punishment.

SEJO: Did you communicate with Tanjong secretly as well?

SERVANT: This baby is to succeed in my former master's family line. But I am merely a poor servant who cannot feed him. I fear that he will starve to death, and my master's noble family will end. I thought it would be better to give him to you. Please spare his life and kill me instead. I dared to break your royal command.

SEJO: Whose son is it?

SERVANT: The grandson of Pak P'aeng-nyŏn, he of the hall of shining wisdom, my Lord.

SHIN SUK-JU: You stand before the king. Tell the truth!

SERVANT: I am an ignorant servant . . . have never known the power of your royal authority.

SHIN SUK-JU: If it be true, you both shall die.

SERVANT: I swear, everything is true.

(Pause.)

SEJO: Come here. Let me look at the child. What is his name?

SERVANT: He has no name yet.

SEJO: What can I do? He came into this world against my orders. He is beyond my power. *(Holding the baby tightly to his chest.)* His hand looks like a branch of coral. So let us name him "One Coral"[8] and let him succeed to the line of Pak, family of the hall of shining wisdom. This is my royal command.

SHIN SUK-JU: Your Majesty! *(Bows low.)*

An Open Field

WIFE: My flesh, my blood. Give me back my flesh. Give him back!
My own flesh.

VOICE: *(Singing Wang's poem.)*

> *I walk into the deep, snowbound forest;*
> *In early summer, one cannot see beneath the ice,*
> *But water is flowing underneath all the same.*
> *Whatever is said of me,*
> *You will fathom my heart, my beloved!*

(The funeral flags flutter in the wind and the sound of a gong is heard.)

NOTES

Lifecord only partially translates the Korean word for the umbilical cord and afterbirth of a child *(t'ae)*.

1. *Zhou Gong* and *King Cheng.* Cheng was the second emperor of China during the Zhou dynasty (1122–255 B.C.), and ascended the throne at an early age requiring his uncle, Zhou Gong, the duke of Zhou, to act as regent for seven years. But, unlike Sejo, the duke relinquished the throne when his nephew came of age. Confucius is said to have respected him for his integrity.

2. *Crows are black.* Several of the poems quoted in the text of *Lifecord* were composed by members of the Sa Yuk Sin, as was this one expressing steadfast devotion to Tanjong. In performance, all the poems in the play are sung by a traditional *p'ansori* performer.

3. *Academy.* This royal academy was the Chiphyŏn-jŏn, founded in 1420 by Sejong, grandfather of Tanjong, for the purpose of studying the Chinese classics. Among the academy's many accomplishments was the creation of *Hangŭl,* the Korean-language writing system, still in use today, and perhaps the most logical major writing system in the world. The Sa Yuk Sin and others (including Shin Suk-ju) were members of this institute. Because of the six scholars' involvement in the 1456 attempt to restore Tanjong to the throne, Sejo closed down the academy.

4. *Ch'ang-ji,* the child's name, is also a word for vital internal organs.

5. *I walk into the deep, snowbound forest.* Wang's poem expresses the hope that, despite surface appearances (the ice), his beloved Tanjong will understand Wang's true feelings of loyalty to his former king (the water flowing underneath).

6. *Saved a pregnant woman's life from murderous sailors.* This is a reference to a historical incident in which Sejo, while still a prince, saved a woman from sailors who tried to sacrifice her to ensure a prosperous voyage. Pak is pointing out that Sejo's actions are inconsistent with his earlier deeds.

7. *Umbilical jar.* An ancient tradition in the Korean court dictated that the umbilical cord and afterbirth of the Crown Prince be kept until his death, when they were ritually buried.

8. *One Coral* translates "Il San."

"They will kill all of my family—parents, children, even newborn babes." Pak Chung-lim's lineage will continue because his servant has sacrificed his infant son to save Pak's unborn grandson.

The ghosts of the Six Scholars haunt Sejo.

Lady Pak gives birth to her son.

Innocently and playfully, Tanjong faces death.

The ghosts of the Six Scholars.

Sejo mourns the death of Tanjong.

WHY DID SHIM CH'ŎNG PLUNGE INTO THE SEA TWICE?

Cast of Characters

SHIM CH'ŎNG

DRAGON KING

SUBJECT *of the Dragon King*

CHŎNG SE-MYŎNG

KU IN-SU

SARGE KIM, *a former soldier*

DETECTIVE

FIREFIGHTER

ASSISTANT *at the Amusement Park*

CUSTOMER

STEERSMAN

YOUNG WOMEN: HŬI-SUN, MI-JŎNG, CHŎNG-HŬI, ŬN-YŎNG,
CH'UN-JA, SŎN-JA, CHŎNG-MIN, KIL-JA, KU-JA, YANG ŬN-SIL,
OK-JA, PAK CHŎNG-SUN

THE WATER PALACE

(SHIM CH'ŎNG *pulls her skirt up over her body and plunges into the water.*
She turns into a butterfly and flies into a submarine where the DRAGON KING
and his SUBJECT *are on board.*)

SUBJECT: Shim Ch'ŏng has arrived safely in the palace!

DRAGON KING: Oh, Shim Ch'ŏng! Welcome! Now there's only one

more step before you can open your father's eyes. Relax, but be discreet.

(*A paperboy passes by, dropping a newspaper. While reading the paper, the* DRAGON KING *abruptly shouts.*)

DRAGON KING: Damn! The world's gone bonkers. Listen to this. A young man kills a woman with a knife just because she asked him to cut his phone call short. The woman was carrying her baby on her back. Bring me my clothes. I've gotta see what's going on in the world.

SHIM CH'ŎNG: I want to go with you.

SUBJECT: She says she wants to come along.

DRAGON KING: Where? You? Not a chance. You're kidding. You're supposed to become an empress.

SHIM CH'ŎNG: But I don't want to.

SUBJECT: What do you mean, you don't want to become an empress? Now wait a second!

SHIM CH'ŎNG: My father said: "You can't enjoy good fortune if you don't deserve it. Never desire other people's treasures."

SUBJECT: Good! That's commendable. Why don't you take her with you? Just to sightsee?

DRAGON KING: No. The world's in a completely different time zone from where you're supposed to wind up. And anyway, it's not the kind of place someone like you should visit. People always getting pissed off, jumping around everywhere like they were in a burning house. Kids bumming cigarettes from old folks. They even buy and sell people like they were cattle. Well, I should get a guide and find out how the world ended up like this. (*To the* SUBJECT.) Find somebody for me. Somebody around thirty, a graduate of an agricultural school, arrived in Seoul in the last three or four years. Someone who wound up being a salesman and is single.

(*The* SUBJECT *manipulates a computer.*)

SUBJECT: I got him. His family name is Chŏng. Chŏng Se-myŏng. Managed a cow shed before he came to Seoul. A healthy young man made in the Republic of Korea. Age twenty-eight. Completed army service. His résumé—Huh? Look at this! I see Shim Ch'ŏng in here, too!

DRAGON KING: What? Why's she in there?

SUBJECT: It says Shim Ch'ŏng's supposed to follow this guy, Chŏng Se-myŏng.

DRAGON KING: What kind of a weird program is that? Well, so where's she supposed to follow him to?

SUBJECT: To a vinyl hothouse. And she sets it on fire.

DRAGON KING: Fire? Fire! But that's dangerous, isn't it?

SUBJECT: Shim Ch'ŏng takes the guy out of a hospital, and then they go to Kunsan.

DRAGON KING: Why to Kunsan?

SUBJECT: Once they're there, they get on a shrimp boat.

DRAGON KING: She gets on a boat again? You mean she jumps into the water again?

SUBJECT: There's no other way she can get back to the water palace.

DRAGON KING: That plot's crazy . . . *(To* SHIM CH'ŎNG.*)* Look, if you're really determined to go, wear a man's clothes. You've got to be real careful not to let anyone know who you are. We're going to a world that's completely different from the one you're used to. So you need to be extremely careful what you say and what you do. I'll say it again: the people up there now aren't like people we're used to. I don't know what's gotten into them. I'm going there to check on it myself, and this young man will be my guide. You still have to become an empress someday, so behave yourself.

SUBJECT: She sure has the morals for one.

DRAGON KING: Basic moral character—that's what people are lacking these days.

A STREET WITH VENDORS

(Street vendors are making a commotion, pulling on customers' sleeves, yelling and hawking cooking pans displayed on their wooden carts. The DRAGON

KING *and* SHIM CH'ŎNG *appear in the midst of the shoppers. The* DRAGON
KING *flashes a bundle of cash, pretending he wants to purchase the pans.
Eventually, some muggers flock around him and grab his money. A street vendor,* CHŎNG SE-MYŎNG, *witnesses the mugging and shouts a warning to the*
DRAGON KING. *One of the muggers is arrested, and the money is returned to
the* DRAGON KING. *However,* SE-MYŎNG *is attacked by one of the muggers
who has been hiding in the crowd. His Achilles tendon is cut, and he is carried to the hospital.*)

DRAGON KING: Let's get out of here.

SHIM CH'ŎNG: We should go to the hospital.

DRAGON KING: What the hell are you babbling about now? Don't be
so old-fashioned. You're a fool to think like that these days.

SHIM CH'ŎNG: But the guy got hurt trying to get your wallet back,
you mean old man.

DRAGON KING: Let's just get out of here. If you talk to the police,
they'll haul us back and forth to the station and ask us all sorts
of questions. It'll be a real hassle.

(*A* DETECTIVE *appears.*)

DETECTIVE: Is that your wallet? How much money you got in it?
Where did you get it? When did the suspect pull out the butcher knife? Show me your exact position at that moment. In such
a dangerous situation—when he could've stuck his knife into
anyone's chest or slashed somebody's neck—how come you
just sat there trying to save your own life? Is that what you call
being a good citizen? How did he handle the knife? Was he like a
butcher or a rice-cake cutter, or was he as good as a sushi chef?

SHIM CH'ŎNG: We should tell him the truth.

DRAGON KING: You think I came up here to catch a lousy thief?

SHIM CH'ŎNG: But the guy got hurt because of us.

DRAGON KING: Do you want to go back to the water?

A Saw-shop Alley

(In a back alley of the East Gate market, saw shops, which offer saw-sharpening services, are lined up. CHŎNG SE-MYŎNG *is seen crawling on the ground like a crocodile while pushing a low-built, wheeled display cart. On the cart are all kinds of paraphernalia such as scrubbing sponges and plumbers' plungers. A saw sharpener,* KU IN-SU, *tries to make a deal with him after choosing a plunger.)*

IN-SU: Does this work good?

SE-MYŎNG: Just give me a dollar.

IN-SU: Wait a minute. Don't I know you? You look familiar.

SE-MYŎNG: I was in the newspaper the other day. "Stabbing Incident at Intersection."

IN-SU: *(Reads the writing scribbled on the side of the cart.)* What's all this about?

SE-MYŎNG: To increase sales, you know. People don't pity me just because I'm crippled.

IN-SU: How much you make a day?

SE-MYŎNG: Enough to feed myself three times a day. That's enough, 'cause I'm just by myself.

IN-SU: Your brain's clogged up. You want me to use this to flush it out? *(He pushes* SE-MYŎNG's *head with a plunger several times. Then he carefully looks around and writes a word down on a piece of paper and shows it to* SE-MYŎNG. *The* DRAGON KING *and* SHIM-CH'ŎNG *watch from a corner.)* You know, people are using these in a lot of different places these days, you follow me?

SE-MYŎNG: Firebombs? . . . yeah, sure they do.

IN-SU: But they're really clamping down now. They changed the law from punishing the users to really punishing the makers and suppliers. On top of that, they have inspections all the time now. So the makers are having a rough time. Then, a light bulb flashed—I came up with a brilliant idea. *(Writes the idea down on a piece of paper to show to* SE-MYŎNG.)*

SE-MYŎNG: Hm. Hm. I heard of a woman who makes big money

selling tear gas,[1] but I didn't know you could make big money in firebombs . . .

IN-SU: No, nobody knows. But to make a long story short, I am offering you a real deal here, a business deal. We can split the profits fifty-fifty. I'll put up the seed money and you take care of sales. *(Writes a contract.)*

DRAGON KING: Oh, no. This guy's rotten to the core. Se-myŏng's having one hell of a year with three disasters hitting him like this. Let's leave him alone and see what he does.

SHIM CH'ŎNG: No, we should help him.

DRAGON KING: We didn't come here to stick our noses in other people's business. We came here on a sight-seeing trip. If you want to have a good time, do it like these people do. Otherwise, we'll have to go back to the sea.

IN-SU: Listen, tonight I'll meet you at Samsongni—the entrance to Pyŏkje—you know where it is, don't you?

SE-MYŎNG: Sure. But what did you say I'd be?

IN-SU: A sales representative.

SE-MYŎNG: A sales representative, eh? Wow!

IN-SU: Put on some warm clothes. We'll be up all night.

(The two men exit.)

DRAGON KING: Did you hear that? These pricks are making firebombs.

SHIM CH'ŎNG: Where's Samsongni?

DRAGON KING: Samsongni's where they have a lot of plastic hothouses. You're supposed to grow vegetables in them, but they use them for some pretty shady operations now.

SHIM CH'ŎNG: But we should stop them from making firebombs.

DRAGON KING: Well, okay then, you could go in there pretending you're a customer and set fire to the hothouse. Do you think you could do that? *(Silence.)* Maybe we should drop the whole thing.

SHIM CH'ŎNG: Is Se-myŏng going to get hurt again?

DRAGON KING: If you want to keep him from going through with it, you've got to scare him off. He may get hurt a little, but at least he'll be alive. Otherwise, a lot of people will get hurt.

SHIM CH'ŎNG: What should I do?

DRAGON KING: Go before anybody else comes in. Pretend to light a cigarette but drop the match on a firebomb. Run away—like it was an accident and you got scared. Don't even look back, just run like hell. You see? Just run.

SHIM CH'ŎNG: Why does Se-myŏng get into so much trouble?

A VINYL HOTHOUSE

(SE-MYŎNG *and* IN-SU *are making firebombs in a vinyl hothouse at Samsongni.*)

SE-MYŎNG: I'm surprised that a good piece of land like this isn't used for farming.

IN-SU: Well, there's a trial going on about it. Anyway, even land needs to rest sometimes.

SE-MYŎNG: But isn't this pretty dangerous?

IN-SU: Dangerous? It's the danger that makes business fun.

SE-MYŎNG: I'm afraid we're not being careful enough.

IN-SU: You know what a barge is? It's like a ferry that carries cargo from an ocean liner to the dock. A barge looks more like a big wooden raft than a boat. Would you believe it if I told you there's a company that had barges carrying rocks from Korea to the Middle East—going almost halfway around the world? The company I'm talking about got a harbor construction deal from one of those rich OPEC countries. And you know a thing like building a harbor needs lots of rocks to begin with. They got lots of sand in the Middle East, but not a damn rock anywhere. So what did they do? Bring in rocks from Korea. But the cost of regular cargo freighters would have made the company go broke. So they decided to use barges. Think of it. Imagine a line of wooden slabs, connected like railroad cars, carrying rocks—

passing through rough weather in the South China Sea, then all the way across the Indian Ocean. And a Korean flag on a tiny, pea-sized mast in the front, waving in the wind. *That's* what I call dangerous.

SE-MYŎNG: But what we're doing can kill people.

IN-SU: *(Ignoring* SE-MYŎNG's *concern.)* And then, a while later, they found a mountain near the construction site where they could get all the rocks they needed. Lucky for the company—they struck it rich. How about that? Is our business worth taking risks for or what? *(*SHIM CH'ŎNG *enters, pretending to be a customer.)* Can I help you?

SHIM CH'ŎNG: I'd like to have this one.

*(*IN-SU *hands* SHIM CH'ŎNG *a firebomb. Her cigarette butt touches the top of the firebomb and sparks begin to fly. The flame spreads through a pile of turpentine bottles and instantly a huge fire erupts.* SE-MYŎNG *rolls on the ground with his hands covering his face.* IN-SU *runs away, and a* FIREFIGHTER *and the* DRAGON KING *enter.)*

FIREFIGHTER: How did this fire start?

SHIM CH'ŎNG: I set the fire.

FIREFIGHTER: You committed arson?

DRAGON KING: That's right, and I encouraged her. I had to do it—a conflict of business, you know.

FIREFIGHTER: You'll have to come with me.

DRAGON KING: Certainly.

SHIM CH'ŎNG: Why did we ever come here? To bring that guy back? It's like he's contagious. Why? Why? Yes, I set the fire. I didn't really understand what it meant when I heard we were coming up here to check on the world. I didn't know it was all about setting fire to an innocent man. Do you know who he is? I only started the fire because *he (indicating the* DRAGON KING*)* said it would only be a warning, just to scare him off, to keep him from getting involved in this filthy business.

DRAGON KING: Geez, I didn't know turpentine was so combustible.

SHIM CH'ŎNG: Listen to him. I know you could have stopped the fire. Why did you let it happen? Why?

A HOSPITAL

(It is the day when SE-MYŎNG *has the gauze removed from his face.*
SHIM CH'ŎNG *is beside him, observing the removal of the bandages.)*

SE-MYŎNG: Ahhhhhhh . . . Ummmmm . . .

SHIM CH'ŎNG: What did you say you used to do for a living?

SE-MYŎNG: I was a street vendor, I already told you.

SHIM CH'ŎNG: I mean, what did you do before you came to Seoul?

SE-MYŎNG: Cows, I raised milking cows. I told you. I had an uncle,
a distant uncle on my mother's side, who raised some three
hundred pigs. After graduating from agricultural high school, I
wasn't doing anything in particular so I helped him out on his
farm. Then he loaned me three calves; told me I could pay him
back when the calves grew up. At first, I was in over my head,
'cause I'd never raised cows before. I'd thought about turning
down his offer at first, but I just couldn't go against my uncle's
wishes. Anyway, I thought, "Hey, what the hell! What do I have
to lose? All I have to do is to let the cows graze for a year." I
thought it wouldn't be much different from raising rabbits. But
it didn't turn out that way. The three cows didn't last the winter, and I had to bury them. Then my mom gave me the deed to
a rice paddy for a new line of business. She must've thought, "A
man shouldn't be discouraged by three dead cows." But I didn't
want to admit defeat, so I bought five cows. I lived for those
cows, sleeping and eating with them. In exactly ten years, I was
making two thousand dollars a month with thirty-three dairy
cows. I was twenty-eight years old then. I was in *New Farmer
Magazine* as one of their success stories. It really was a glorious
success for a country boy like me.

　　Do you remember when the Kŭm River flooded last year?
Only three or four months after my success, that damned flood
came. It swept away everything—cows, cow shed, refrigeration
equipment, milking machines. It washed away everything. I was
standing there, staring at the ugly, red dirt covering everything

I owned when I suddenly remembered what the martyr Yun Pong-gil[2] said—"Now I'm leaving home. If I were a real man, I'd never come back alive." I was never able to figure out what he meant until that moment. He said that just when he'd lost everything, his money, even his country. So I thought to myself, "My life shouldn't depend on thirty-three cows. All right, then, I'll forget about them." I left home, no money in my pocket, all by myself, without even saying good-bye to my mom. So here I am, floating around in the world. Well, I let my pathetic little story go on too long, didn't I? By the way, when will the old man get out of prison?

SHIM CH'ŎNG: At the end of the month.

SE-MYŎNG: I don't see why he has to stay in prison so long. He's an old man, after all, and, anyway, how can they keep him in such an awful place?

SHIM CH'ŎNG: Awful place? Don't worry about him. He says it's fun to be around so many "interesting" people. By the way, have you looked at your face? I'm worried whether you can make it with a face like that.

SE-MYŎNG: Why, what's wrong with my face? *(Indicating a box containing nine balls of different colors,* SE-MYŎNG *gives* SHIM CH'ŎNG *a wooden hammer to hit the balls with.)* You want to try?

(Thinking it a joke, SHIM CH'ŎNG *half-heartedly hits the balls with the wooden hammer. As she hits the balls, a voice of a child is heard from the box repeatedly screaming, "Why are you hitting me? It hurts. Hit me again.")*

SE-MYŎNG: This game is like printing money. When the doctor goes around the patients' beds in the morning, a boy always follows him, carrying this box. I have no idea how he does it, but the kid picks a patient, gives him the hammer, and stares at him. Like a zombie, the patient grabs the hammer and beats the shit out of the box, yelling, "I'll never die. Why should I die? I'll never die! Why should I be the one? No one else has to go except me? No, never. I'll never die!" They yell and scream beating this thing, but I've never seen one patient refuse to play the game. Sure, they have to pay the boy to play—I found out he's making more money than a cab driver, you know. "Why should I die? Why?" I learned an important lesson from that kid. I found a way to live my life.

(Stage assistants who have been acting as nurse's aides quickly change the scenery from a hospital room into an amusement park. A sign is hung over the stage that reads, "See the Moving Human Target, The White Mask." SE-MYŎNG *appears wearing a white mask made from a construction worker's helmet. To attract customers, his* ASSISTANT *shouts and throws balls at* SE-MYŎNG, *The White Mask.)*

ASSISTANT: Get read——y and shoot! Only two dollars for ten balls! But please, no rocks. Remember, "Who will cast the first stone at this woman?"

(Each time a ball hits the target, blood pumps from holes in SE-MYŎNG'*s mask and heart.)*

SE-MYŎNG: My future's bright! I'll make enough money to buy cows!

SHIM CH'ŎNG: Make money to buy cows!

SE-MYŎNG: I'll buy thirty-three cows and ride home in glory.

SHIM CH'ŎNG: Cows, cows, cows!

SE-MYŎNG: Cows, cows, cows!

SHIM CH'ŎNG VISITS THE DRAGON KING IN PRISON

*(*SHIM CH'ŎNG *holds a flower in her hands and speaks to it.)*

SHIM CH'ŎNG: I had a dream about him last night—a bad dream. Now that he's been put away for so long, he must be lonely. I'm afraid he'll get sick just a few days before he's released. In the meantime, you've got to comfort him for me. Here he comes.

DRAGON KING: You come here everyday. I'm glad to see you. I hear I have only a few more days to go. Eight more days or something like that, isn't it? I think I should put off my release from prison, though—for another month or so. You should arrange that for me.

SHIM CH'ŎNG: Put off your release?

DRAGON KING: An amazing guy came in just yesterday. *(Pulling out a deck of cards.)* He taught me this card game. It's called "Trump," and everybody falls for it. *(Quoting an old proverb.)* "In time of plenty, prepare for want." Who knows, this trick may come in handy some day. It's also a good way to pass the time.

SHIM CH'ŏNG: You mean you want to put off getting out of jail just to learn card tricks?

DRAGON KING: But learning can take place anywhere. There's no age limit for learning, you know.

SHIM CH'ŏNG: Oh, sure. Why not? Learn how to use sushi knives, how to pick people's pockets, how to make firebombs, how to swindle and gamble, how to commit forgery and carjackings. Learn everything you can. If you need more than a month, take your time. Doesn't matter if it's a year or ten years. *(Changing tone.)* Please, stop this nonsense, and get out on time. I can't stand to see Se-myŏng suffer anymore. He's just out of the hospital, but I can't help him. You have to get out of the prison to help him.

DRAGON KING: Oh, that's right, they've taken the bandages off of Se-myŏng's face. How's he look? Are his eyes, nose, and mouth all in the right place?

SHIM CH'ŏNG: He's what they call "The Moving Human Target"— he gets hit every day with tennis balls.

DRAGON KING: Who throws the balls? I don't get it.

SHIM CH'ŏNG: I can't even look at it, it's so horrible. It's inhuman. He covers his mangled face with a safety helmet and gets hit with balls. Then he dances around saying, "Why are you hitting me? It hurts, it hurts. But hit me again." Day in and day out, he dances and screams, "It hurts. But hit me again."

DRAGON KING: That's it. I knew it. I knew he'd turn out fine no matter what. His future looks promising. He's doing a good job 'cause he doesn't get discouraged. The man who walks alone is strongest . . .

SHIM CH'ŏNG: I'm going back to the Water Palace. I'm sorry I ever came along on this trip.

(Exits.)

DRAGON KING: Where do you think you're going? You sure you know your way back?

VOICE OF SHIM CH'ŎNG: I'll jump in the water from a boat—oh, no, the sharks could get me!

DRAGON KING: You'll do no such thing. You'll mess up the plan. Come on, Shim Ch'ŏng. Nobody knows we came up here. If anyone finds out, I'll lose my throne. Shim Ch'ŏng-ah! Get me out of here in eight days. I'll give up cards. Shim Ch'ŏng-ah! Ch'ŏng! Please help me. Hey, guard! Let me out of here. She's drowning. Our Shim Ch'ŏng is dying! Help! Let me out! Someone! Anyone?

THE AMUSEMENT PARK

(The scene returns to the amusement park. To the sign "See the Moving Human Target, The White Mask" has been added the word, "Original." SE-MYŎNG *is sitting precariously on top of a water tank. A drunken* CUSTOMER *enters.)*

CUSTOMER: Hey! Write the name Kim Kwang-sŏn on his name tag. You bastard! I'll kill you today! I will kill you and kill you and kill you. *(To* SE-MYŎNG's *assistant.)* Hey, what're you doing? I told you to write down the name and put it around the guy's neck. I said, put the name tag around his neck!

ASSISTANT: We can't do that sort of thing here. Please go away.

CUSTOMER: Where to? What the fuck is your problem? All I'm asking is to write down this name—three lousy words—on a name tag, you asshole. Then I'm going to beat Kim Kwang-sŏn to death. Kim Kwang-sŏn, Kim Kwang-sŏn.

ASSISTANT: Go next door. We don't have name tags.

CUSTOMER: You son of a bitch! Do as I say! Put on the mask, and do as I say, you bastard!

(He knocks the ASSISTANT *down.* SE-MYŎNG *glares at the customer. Intimidated by The White Mask, the* CUSTOMER *exits. In one corner of the*

stage is SHIM CH'ŎNG. *She wears a white mask that she has picked up from a street vendor.*)

SHIM CH'ŎNG: It's incredible! Everybody's wearing a white mask now. People probably saw it on TV the other night. Today the guy who sells white masks was swamped by people. "The Human Target, The White Mask, The Moving Target—only two dollars." It's such a great idea. But don't forget who threw the balls the first time. By the way, why's he standing there like that? Is he sick?

ASSISTANT: He says he is going to close down the business.

SHIM CH'ŎNG: How come? Everyone's crazy about the game since they showed it on TV.

ASSISTANT: TV ruined the whole thing.

SHIM CH'ŎNG: How did it get on TV, anyway?

ASSISTANT: It happened the other day. A young guy spends a good half day here watching the game. Says what fun it is. Then he suggests that Se-myŏng go on television—but with a condition. Says that since it gets boring to show the same scene for more than three minutes, Se-myŏng should wear a dog tag to add variety.

SHIM CH'ŎNG: A dog tag?

ASSISTANT: Don't you know those name tags criminals have to wear around their necks? He wanted Se-myŏng to wear one of those.

SHIM CH'ŎNG: So Se-myŏng becomes a wanted criminal?

ASSISTANT: Listen. Let's say there's a certain son of a bitch you've always wanted to beat the shit out of, say his name's Joe Schmuck. So you write "Joe Schmuck" on a name tag, hang it around Se-myŏng's neck, and throw balls at him. Don't you see, it's just like real and it helps to relieve stress. It's great, isn't it? But guess what? Se-myŏng refused the guy's offer flat. Says "I don't do dog tags." Just like that.

SHIM CH'ŎNG: So who'd they show on TV then?

ASSISTANT: Aw, they dressed up some guy at the TV station—there's lots of different people there.

SHIM CH'ŎNG: (*To* SE-MYŎNG.) But what did you tell me in the hospital? Didn't you say you'd found a way to live with that face? Didn't you say that it wouldn't be a problem to live? Didn't you? Cows! Thirty-three of them. Milking cows, cows, cows!

ASSISTANT: He says he doesn't like this business.

SHIM CH'ŎNG: But didn't he invent the moving target?

ASSISTANT: But he thinks it's no fun anymore to put a name on the tag around his neck.

SHIM CH'ŎNG: But it's entertainment. It's what the customers want.

(*A loud hubbub of people is heard from one corner of the stage.*)

SHIM CH'ŎNG: Listen to them. They're having a great time. *Their businesses are booming.*

(*At this moment the previous customer reenters. A name tag with Kim Kwang-sŏn written on it is now hanging around his neck.*)

SHIM CH'ŎNG: Welcome! Two bucks for ten balls at The Moving Human Target!

CUSTOMER: Hey, hang this around the guy's neck. (*Giving* SHIM CH'ŎNG *the name tag, he buys a basketful of balls for the game.* SHIM CH'ŎNG *hangs the name tag around* SE-MYŎNG's *neck. The* CUSTOMER *starts throwing the balls while yelling loudly.*) You son of a bitch! You should be ashamed of yourself. Shut up! You asshole! I'm talking to you now. How dare you keep on talking. (*Throws balls. Each time the ball hits* SE-MYŎNG's *body, blood gushes out from holes at the top of his head and on his chest. The* CUSTOMER *buys two more baskets of balls. When he runs out of balls, he yells at the* ASSISTANT.) Hey! Bring more balls here! Can't you see I've run out? Pick up the balls and bring them over here!

(*The* ASSISTANT *crawls on the ground picking up balls to put into the basket. He collects the balls floating in the water tank.*)

CUSTOMER: You son of a bitch! Do you have any idea how grateful I was to you at first? When you said we should give each other our reports and take them home for a final check before turning them in, I trusted you. You asshole! I thought you were looking out for me. I was so thankful, I even felt sorry that I'd ever thought the world was rotten. I thought this world was just fine, because there were still people like you in it. Bastard! If you'd told me that day to jump off the tallest building in Seoul,[3] I would have done it for you. I mean, I really respected you and trusted you. Then what did you do with it? You threw it back in my face. I am not talking about the report anymore, you son of a bitch! I'm not interested in the money. Just listen to that asshole, I'd like to kill him. I don't care about the report you stole anymore. Goddamned, mother-fucker from hell! I wouldn't have thought twice about jumping into the Han River to kill myself for you. Do you understand what that means? I felt really good that I could trust you. I said I don't want your money! Don't you have anything to say besides that? You damn asshole! You, come here! *(Picks up a shovel that has been placed in one corner.)*

ASSISTANT: Please, sir, you'll never win a prize this way.

CUSTOMER: Why did you lie? You slimeball! Shut your mouth, asshole! Shut up!

(He strikes the ASSISTANT *with the shovel. Clutching his head, the* ASSISTANT *runs away screaming. The* CUSTOMER *follows the* ASSISTANT, *yelling and striking him with the shovel. A loud scream is heard and then subsides. The* CUSTOMER *returns with a bloody shovel. He then approaches* SE-MYŎNG. SHIM CH'ŎNG, *letting out a sharp cry, blocks the* CUSTOMER's *way. She picks up the balls and, screaming, hurls them at the* CUSTOMER.)

SHIM CH'ŎNG: Go away! Go! Get out of here!

CUSTOMER: All right, all right. That hurts. I'll stop. I give up. I've lost.

(The CUSTOMER *throws down the shovel and exits. Enter the* DRAGON KING.)

DRAGON KING: Congratulations! Looks like The Moving Human Target has a bright future. Look at all this! Wow, it's really festive, huh? What's this? Blood? *(He exits briefly to look at the* ASSISTANT *and then comes back.)* He's dead.

SE-MYŎNG: *(Taking off the name tag from his neck and throwing it away.)* I never wanted a sign around my neck in the first place.

SHIM CH'ŎNG: Wait a minute. You've no place to go to but here. I only put it around your neck to keep your business going. I wanted you to do well here. *(Picking up the name tag and hanging it back around his neck.)* The Moving Human Target! Get ready and shoot! Remember? Martyr Yun Pong-gil. Cows. Thirty-three of them. Milking cows. Why are you hitting me? It hurts. Ouch, ouch! But please hit me again. Cows. Martyr Yun Pong-gil. Ouch! Ouch! Hit me again. Why are they hitting me? Cows. Cows. Cows. Cows. Cows. Martyr Yun Pong-gil. Ouch! Cows, please hit me again, cows, cows, cows, martyr Yun Pong-gil, cows, cows, cows . . .

SE-MYŎNG: *(Making cow horns with his fingers on either side of his forehead.)* I keep forgetting them. I think I should put horns right here so I don't forget the cows. Hey, let's go get the cows, all right?

SHIM CH'ŎNG: Let's go get the cows.

*(*SHIM CH'ŎNG *throws balls at* SE-MYŎNG, *who, ignoring them, starts jumping around frantically. Blood gushes out so forcefully from him that it seems to pour out in buckets from the holes on top of his headgear and on his chest.* SE-MYŎNG's *body shakes for a while as if he were having an epileptic fit, then he collapses sideways on the ground. He breathes heavily.)*

SHIM CH'ŎNG: *(To the* DRAGON KING.*)* Do something, please! Help him stop.

DRAGON KING: Have you ever been on board a ship? Why don't we go fishing? In Kunsan, there are lots of shrimp boats. I met this guy in prison who's from Kunsan, and he was making a killing there. So I lined up a boat for us. If you work one season and then, at the end of the season, sell the boat—you'll make more than enough money for thirty-three cows. Let's get on board!

SE-MYŎNG: *(Taking off his mask.)* Let's get on board!

DRAGON KING: Let's get on board!

CHANGHANG

(While squatting on the edge of a landing pier, the DRAGON KING *sends a secret code to the Water World through a hand-held transmitter.)*

DRAGON KING: "Spider, bitsy, itsy. Spout climbed up the water."

(A ship named Snapping Turtle *emerges from the ocean manipulated by the* DRAGON KING'S SUBJECT.*)*

SUBJECT: "Bitsy, itsy, sun. Went down the drain again."

DRAGON KING: Look, I see the big smokestack of the Changhang Refinery rising up into the sky. I'm facing Kunsan Port. What's the location of my shrimp boat? Roger.

SUBJECT: This is *Snapping Turtle.* I'm at north-northwest, forty meters from Kunsan pier; water, five meters deep. I can see you through the periscope. Keep going south.

DRAGON KING: Keep going south? We'll drown in the Kŭm River, you idiot! You said, according to the scenario, a shrimp boat would be waiting for me at Kunsan. I followed your directions, dragging Shim Ch'ŏng and this guy with the ugly face all the way down here in a little boat called *Unification.* And, now you're telling me to keep going south where I'll drown in the water? Is that all you can say?

SUBJECT: Then don't go south. Take a ferry.

DRAGON KING: And?

SUBJECT: Your cellmate in prison tore a ten-dollar bill in two and gave half to you. Do you still have it? *(The* DRAGON KING *takes it out of his pocket.)* Go to Kunsan pier, fish market number 12, and look for a pimp named Sarge—Sergeant Kim. You can be sure he's the right guy if the two pieces of the bill fit together. As soon as you're certain, pay him the rest of the money and he'll hand over a small coastal liner, the *Sea Gull F27.*

DRAGON KING: *Sea Gull F27!* My shrimp boat!

SUBJECT: Pick up a load of boxes at the fish market and get to the West Sea as soon as you can.

DRAGON KING: Boxes? It's better to put shrimp into pots. Pickled shrimp go in pots.

SUBJECT: You're not dealing with shrimp. You're dealing with flowers. You know, "flowers of the night."

DRAGON KING: What did you say? Night? Light? What night?

SUBJECT: You're supposed to be a pimp.

DRAGON KING: Pimp? You slime! How dare you get me involved in something like that! You scum!—Wait! A pimp? *(Giggles.)* He, he, he, he. I like that. But what do I do with the shrimp boat?

SUBJECT: Shrimp fishing is too rough for an old man like you.

DRAGON KING: But I promised this young guy we'd get a shrimp boat. I can't break my word, not at my age.

SUBJECT: The scenario has changed.

DRAGON KING: Who changed it?

SUBJECT: Scenario subject to change.

DRAGON KING: Well, anyway, I like being a pimp better than a shrimp fisherman. The girls are pretty, aren't they?

SUBJECT: Would you do something with them if they're good-looking?

DRAGON KING: Me? Nah! I was just thinking about business prospects—you see, they have to be pretty to sell. And they need to sell so I can get my investment back.

SUBJECT: But you don't get your money back. The girls all jump into the sea.

DRAGON KING: The sea? You mean they wind up like Shim Ch'ŏng? Oh, no, they're too young to end their lives in the cold ocean— no, they shouldn't do that!

SUBJECT: Do you want to follow the program or not?

DRAGON KING: But why do we have to sacrifice these girls—especially when they're so pretty? Didn't you say they were? No, I can't allow it—only over my dead body!

SUBJECT: If you mess up the scenario, I'll have to take over your position.

DRAGON KING: Position? I don't give a damn about that. You can have it. But not the girls.

SUBJECT: I hope you don't regret this later. "Spider, bitsy itsy. Went down the drain again!"

(The SUBJECT *disappears.)*

A FISH MARKET

(At a fish market "women of the night" are on display in rows of cardboard boxes like fish for sale. Beside each box, pimps are hawking for customers. Several young men choose women they like and make a deal for them. The Dragon King is looking around with curiosity. SHIM CH'ŎNG *and* SE-MYŎNG *are busy taking pictures. The* DRAGON KING *takes out a half of the torn bill and shows it around until he finally meets the* SARGE, *who has the other half of the bill. The* DRAGON KING *hands a bundle of bills to the* SARGE, *who pushes aside a sign for the fish market to reveal the mast of the* Sea Gull F27.*)*

SARGE: The engine was made in Germany, and it works like a dream.

DRAGON KING: *(Indicating the boxes in which the girls are seated.)* Are those the boxes you want us to carry? According to my Subject, we're supposed to carry boxes.

SARGE: Yeah, forty-seven. I carefully chose them out of over two thousand.

DRAGON KING: Forty seven? Forty-seven people will jump into the water? That's a massacre! I can't go along with that. *(Taking the* SARGE *into a corner.)* Look, I've got a problem. The two kids with me think they're coming on a shrimp boat. They'll make trouble if they find out the boat deal has changed. I mean, they'll probably try to back out of the contract.

SARGE: Back out of the contract?

DRAGON KING: Well, maybe not. But I wish I had a good excuse for why I had to switch boats.

SARGE: That's no problem. Let's do it like this. Why don't you pick a quarrel and make a scene? Hey, you! Come over here! Take care of this old man's complaints.

DRAGON KING: Make a scene? That's easy. Well, let's see. I guess I'm trying to see how to get these women on board. I bought myself a shrimp boat and I need . . . some women who can . . . process salted shrimp.

HŬI-SUN: Lover boy, you're drunk.

SARGE: Hey, we don't have any shrimp. Go somewhere else.

DRAGON KING: Come on, the customer is king. How can you treat a customer like this?

SHIM CH'ŎNG: *(To the* SARGE, *defending the* DRAGON KING.*)* He's an old man. He must have misunderstood you. If you tell it to me straight, I can make him understand . . .

SARGE: Straight, you say? What do you mean by that, you bitch!

(The SARGE *strikes* SHIM CH'ŎNG, *who collapses and rolls on the ground.* HŬI-SUN *covers* SHIM CH'ŎNG'S *body with a huge cardboard box and pushes it offstage. All of a sudden,* SE-MYŎNG *realizes that* SHIM CH'ŎNG *is missing.)*

SE-MYŎNG: Old man! The boxes! Make sure they don't steal the boxes! If we lose them, we'll never find Shim Ch'ŏng! Make sure they don't move any of these boxes!

*(*SE-MYŎNG *rummages through the boxes. The* DRAGON KING *grabs* TU-CH'WI, *a dock worker by his neck, threatening to strangle him, and yells.)*

DRAGON KING: Put the boxes on the boat! If you don't, I'll kill myself and Se-myŏng. Get them on the boat! Don't stand there looking at me. Start moving. Right now!

(Popular songs are heard from the fish market. Workers carry the boxes.)

DRAGON KING: Stand by to launch the ship! Go forward! Forward!

SE-MYŎNG: Forward!

(One can hear the sound of a fog horn and the engine running, signifying that the Sea Gull F27 *is leaving Kunsan pier through the early-morning fog with forty-six cardboard boxes visible on its rear deck.)*

DRAGON KING: Full speed ahead!

SE-MYŎNG: Where to?

DRAGON KING: First, let's get away from those slimy characters. What are they doing with those girls? How can they do that to human beings? They treat them like they're fish in the market, don't they? Good god, they keep the girls cooped up like chickens in a cage. Damned bastards!

SE-MYŎNG: *(Looking for* SHIM CH'ŎNG.*)* I don't see her. Are you sure you didn't leave her box on the pier?

DRAGON KING: Look around everywhere. Go under the front deck
     to the engine room. She's got to be here. She came on board, so
     she must be somewhere on the ship.
     (SE-MYŎNG *takes a break after looking through the boxes.*)
SE-MYŎNG: Hey, gramps, how are you related to the girl?
DRAGON KING: Which girl? Oh, Shim Ch'ŏng? Oh, she's a distant,
     distant niece on my mother's side. Her family name's Shim—of
     the Shim Tal-lae clan. Her given name is Ch'ŏng, which means
     "blue." So, together, her name's Shim Ch'ŏng. To find her, call
     out, "Shim Ch'ŏng-ah! Shim Ch'ŏng-ah!"
SE-MYŎNG: How old is she?
DRAGON KING: (*Sensing* SE-MYŎNG's *attraction to* SHIM CH'ŎNG.) Don't!
     Not you. Uh, uh. Not for you. She's already engaged to . . .
     someone else. Don't even think about it. She's a precious thing
     who will become an empress—Er, uh . . . I mean, you should
     never think of her as your——
SE-MYŎNG: I didn't mean that.
DRAGON KING: No, I won't let you be her—over my dead body.
SE-MYŎNG: It's not that I want her. But she and you have done so
     much for a guy like me. You two make me feel like life is still
     worth living. When I make enough money for the cows—work-
     ing on this shrimp boat—I'll pay you back. You know, old man,
     our shrimp boat is really something, isn't it? It sails so smooth.
DRAGON KING: Shrimp, shrimp. God, do you have any idea what
     you're talking about? Shrimping is the hardest kind of fishing
     there is. Most fishermen don't want anything to do with
     shrimp. Only a certain kind of man gets on a shrimp boat. And
     most people avoid any kind of fishing in the first place, because
     the work's too hard and dangerous. I've seen a lot of bums sleep-
     ing in bus terminals and train stations shanghaied to an island
     and sold as fishermen. In other words, they grab guys who don't
     have anywhere else to go and put them to work on shrimp
     boats. Anyhow, once you get on shrimp boat, you never come
     back. It's the same with these girls—once you step on Hŭksan

Island everybody knows you never escape. Hey, girls, this is your world now. Enjoy yourselves.

(The girls, who have now changed into simple and comfortable clothes, sit in a row on the deck and start singing.)

SE-MYŎNG: I'll work hard and buy cows with the money I make. I'm not afraid of working on a shrimp boat. It can't be that hard. I hear the people on the island do the work. Sure, I can do it. No problem.

MI-JŎNG: If we can make a living, there's no reason you shouldn't be able to do anything you want—so long as you're healthy.

CHŎNG-HŬI: Keep your hopes up.

ŬN-YŎNG: Don't be afraid of anything—you're young. Catch all the shrimp you can. All of them!

SE-MYŎNG: Let's catch shrimp to buy cows!

CH'UN-JA: What? Catch cows?

CHŎNG-MIN: He means we'll catch shrimp, sell them at the market, and then buy cows with the money.

SE-MYŎNG: Let's catch shrimp and make tons of pickled shrimp.

CH'UN-JA: Wash the shrimp clean.

ŬN-YŎNG: Pour salt on them.

CHŎNG-MIN: I'll handle the salt.

MI-JŎNG: Get jars.

CHŎG-HŬI: We'll pack the little shrimps in the bottom of the jar.

ŬN-YŎNG: Barley shrimp—they're called that because they're plump like little barleycorns.

CHŎNG-MIN: Put the medium-sized, fat ones in the middle.

MI-JŎNG: And cover the top with tiny shrimps.

SE-MYŎNG: Let's sell pickled shrimp and buy cows. One cow——

EVERYONE: Thirty-two cows, forty-three cows, fifty-three cows, sixty-five cows, seventy-six cows, eighty-seven cows, ninety-eight cows——

(The idea that they can make money by working hard as fishermen makes all of them excited and proud of themselves.)

SE-MYŎNG: Let's go fishing for shrimp.

EVERYONE: *(Singing a children's song.)* "Shall we go to the sea and catch shrimp? Shall we go to the river and catch shrimp?"

DRAGON KING: Forget it. Forget it. We don't need to work that hard. We can make money a lot easier than that.

SE-MYŎNG: Now how do we make easy money with this boat?

DRAGON KING: You know there're lots of single guys in little farming villages, don't you? Can you imagine how many of them there are in these islands? All the girls have left for the big cities, and there aren't any women for the men. Now, *we* have girls— on average, seventeen, eighteen years old. So, I'm saying that we sail around these islands with forty-seven girls on board.

SE-MYŎNG: We sail through these islands on the boat?

DRAGON KING: The scheduled trip should take four nights and five days. We begin with Hŭksan Island, and then take in all the islands in the West Sea, the South Sea, and the East Sea. It'll be a fun trip. In the meantime, we'll perform a charitable service for the men in the islands. In other words, this boat will be like a Red Cross ship.

SE-MYŎNG: For how long?

DRAGON KING: Four months.

(SE-MYŎNG *lets out a violent laugh and almost chokes while laughing. The girls shout for joy and make a lot of noise while hoisting the* DRAGON KING *shoulder-high.*)

DRAGON KING: A Red Cross vessel hoists a red flag, I hear. Why don't we hang up a yellow one for our boat?

SE-MYŎNG: You mean we should raise a flag?

DRAGON KING: Sure. But, girls, you need to raise your own flags, too. Fly a different flag from each one of your boxes. It'll look splendid from a distance. People will think it's a flower boat. Yeah, they'll respond to a flower boat.

(*Emitting a sharp cry,* SE-MYŎNG *jumps at the* DRAGON KING. *After swiftly dodging the attack, the* DRAGON KING *opens the cover of a box that was placed in one corner.*)

DRAGON KING: Shim Ch'ŏng-ah! Everything's all right now. We've sailed out on the high seas, leaving behind those jerks on shore. You can come out now.

(SHIM CH'ŎNG *appears. The girls are joyful to see her.*)

SHIM CH'ŎNG: Where are we going?

DRAGON KING: We're on a sight-seeing tour.

SHIM CH'ŎNG: Are the girls with us? That's great!

(SE-MYŎNG *takes* SHIM CH'ŎNG *into a corner.*)

SE-MYŎNG: (*To* SHIM CH'ŎNG.) Look, the old man isn't interested in fishing for shrimp. He said he's planning to take these girls on a tour of the islands. For four months, these women will . . . will . . .

SHIM CH'ŎNG: That's a good idea. I saw these girls sitting in boxes a while ago, and it reminded me of my first sacrifice on a boat.

DRAGON KING: (*Holding a flag in one hand, leads* SHIM CH'ŎNG *to the prow.*) A flag is important. But we shouldn't use any old piece of dirty cotton. There should be hundreds of flags in all different colors, like a bouquet, all decorated with gold fringe. Then, when this boat of flowers appears on the horizon, men on the islands will ask, "What's that?" Let's say, one flag belongs to a girl named Ch'un-ja. And let's imagine Ch'un-ja visits a guy named Tŏk-sang. Each time the flag waves in the wind, Tŏk-sang will think of it as Ch'un-ja waving her handkerchief at him, saying, "Here I am! Your Ch'un-ja has come back to you!" Now, let's say we're coming up on Ullŭng Island. On this island, Yŏng-ja and Kŭm-ja are popular. So we hoist their flags to the top of the mast. If it's Chakyak Island and the oldest or the youngest girls are popular there, then it'll be *their* flags flying in the wind. Do you see what I am saying? Even for unpopular girls that don't sell well, we can still make money by lending them out to bars and taverns on the island. We'll hang the flags of the unpopular girls at the end of the boat. That way, the girls will see clearly how they're doing—whether they go to the top of the mast or they trail behind at the back of the boat. Let's say one of the girls finds her flag hanging on the stern end; she'll go crazy. Hee, hee.

Wouldn't she work her butt off to get to the top? *(Handing* SHIM CH'ŏNG *a flag.)* This is yours. This flag will fly at the top of the mast.

SHIM CH'ŏNG: Oh no, it'll probably go at the back.

DRAGON KING: Don't be modest—or you'll be left at one of the taverns on the island. Work hard and make sure you do better than the other girls. Practice. Sing after me. *(Sings a traditional Korean folk song and encourages* SHIM CH'ŏNG *and the other girls to sing along with him.)*

(Boxes, which have been placed in a row upstage, open up simultaneously, revealing the girls sitting in them. They all sing the song together, waving their flags along with the DRAGON KING. SHIM CH'ŏNG *climbs into the box assigned to her and, waving her flag, joins in the song.* SE-MYŏNG *drags the* DRAGON KING *to the bow of the boat and points to the horizon in the distance.)*

SE-MYŏNG: Human beings talk to dogs. We speak to cats. We also talk to cows, goats, grasshoppers, horses, chickens, even pigeons. Fabre spoke to an insect,[4] my mom talks to a toad, and my younger brother even talks to a goldbug. But people don't talk to leeches, or to mosquitoes, fleas, and blood-sucking lice. I don't want to talk to you, you asshole!

*(*SE-MYŏNG *strangles the* DRAGON KING. *After a while, he pushes the* DRAGON KING's *body over the railing into the sea. Water splashes upward. Utterly shocked, the girls stop singing.* SHIM CH'ŏNG *runs to the railing and looks down at the ocean. She murmurs, as if speaking to herself.)*

SHIM CH'ŏNG: *(To the ocean.)* Serves you right. In fact, it's a big relief. I feel much better now that you're gone. I think I'll have fun traveling with these people a little longer. So . . . see you soon.

(Hearing SHIM CH'ŏNG *speak in this way,* SE-MYŏNG *assumes that she has lost her mind from shock.* SE-MYŏNG *speeds up his plan.)*

SE-MYŏNG: *(To the girls, as if they were children.)* You're all very pretty. I'll let you go home now. You're young; you should play like kids are supposed to. Have fun! Eat well, grow healthy, get married, and have kids in a nice little house in the woods . . . *(Stepping up on the bow.)* Hey, steersman!

STEERSMAN: I'm here.

SE-MYŏNG: How far can we reach with our radio?

STEERSMAN: We can transmit from the east end all the way to the south. Kunsan? No problem.

SE-MYŏNG: Send the following message. "From the *Sea Gull F27*, on the high seas, Kunsan area. A notorious criminal has kidnapped forty-seven girls and insists on holding a press conference." Date is today; time, two o'clock; location, the deck of the *Sea Gull*. And, let them know the ship's location as it appears on the chart. Get going!

STEERSMAN: Yes, sir!

SE-MYŏNG: *(To the girls.)* You'll be on TV tonight.

CH'UN-JA: Oh, my gosh. Let's put on some makeup. Hey, girls, put on some makeup.

SE-MYŏNG: Myŏng Ch'un-ja! Step to the bow.

CH'UN-JA: Okay. *(Steps to the bow.)*

SE-MYŏNG: When your face appears on television, tell the viewers how much you owe your pimp as of today. Then somebody watching will pity you and promise to pay off your debts and save you.

CH'UN-JA: *(Sarcastically.)* Oh, sure. I believe that. A guy will rescue me from here, for sure.

SE-MYŏNG: It'll be different. I promise. This time, you'll go home.

CH'UN-JA: They always say that to get us to do what they want.

SE-MYŏNG: But I guarantee it.

(Everyone whoops for joy.)

SE-MYŏNG: But to make it come true, I need to know a couple of things about you. What is your assigned beat?

CH'UN-JA: Kunsan, the second pier, association 6, joint market, display stand B, number D 2027. Name, Myŏng Ch'un-ja, resident registration number, 123456-654321.

SE-MYŏNG: How much are you in debt?

CH'UN-JA: You gonna pay it off for me? No one, even those who like to stick their nose in our business, has ever paid off a cent of my debt. Why should I squeal it to you?

(SE-MYŎNG *steps on* CH'UN-JA'S *foot.*)

CH'UN-JA: Ouch! Okay, all right! . . . It's not so much. I owe 200 dollars to the beauty parlor . . . *(Still feeling pain on her foot.)* Ouch! It
still hurts. What did you do that for? Okay, okay, I'll tell you.
The car payment is 120 dollars a month. It's a red Hyundai
Scoupe. It's the only pleasure I have in life. I haven't got a driver's license yet—the engine stalled out going up a hill.
Anyway, I owe 100 dollars to the drug store. I'm not sure, but I
think I owe this woman we call Mi-ae's mom about 500 dollars.
I'll have to look at my account book to make sure. For makeup,
I got 450 dollars to pay over fourteen months; and another debt
for makeup is around 200 for eight months. I have 50 dollars left
to pay to the credit union, and 3,500 to another credit union.
Then there's 3,000 and more than 6,000 dollars due to my mutu-
al-loan club's travel savings plans. I'm going to go to Europe and
Hokkaido. Do you know how nice the hot springs are in
Hokkaido? I still owe 57 dollars on the stereo system. I haven't
paid the mortgage on the condominium, that's 250 dollars. I
joined up with some other girls to rent this condo apartment for
our trip. It was much less expensive than staying in a hotel. See,
a hotel room would have cost more than twice what we paid for
the condo. Well, including the 5,000 I borrowed from my pimp,
the total is 15,066 dollars.

SE-MYŎNG: What did you borrow the money from the pimp for?

CH'UN-JA: Oh, well, you think I should walk around naked then?

SE-MYŎNG: Next!

CH'UN-JA: By the way, do you really think someone will call? Who'd
show up for a person like me?

SE-MYŎNG: Somebody will. Otherwise, you'll die.

CH'UN-JA: What are you talking about? How can you say such a
nasty thing?

SE-MYŎNG: Well, who made you like this? It's *them*, isn't it?

CH'UN-JA: That's right.

SE-MYŎNG: Yes. You're their responsibility. If they refuse to take
responsibility for you, you should have enough pride to leave

this filthy world. Say, "All right, I quit," and then jump into the middle of the ocean.

CH'UN-JA: You're right. Hmm, it's getting serious, isn't it?

SE-MYŎNG: Next!

KIL-JA: So if some saint who'll pay my debts doesn't turn up, I get to call off this crummy life—is that it? Well, that's a bit much! But, at this point, let me at least tell you what's on my mind.

(Despite its melodramatic content, this speech is shouted to the audience in a confrontational style by the male actor who plays this role.)

My name is Wang Kil-ja, abandoned by the world, standing here at the bow. I'm only twenty years old. As I take off my shoes and put them in the corner to get ready to jump overboard,[5] I look for the moon, hiding in the clouds. Dear moon, please light my way. I can't see in the dark. My sweaty hair, which stuck to my forehead, now blows in the wind. It blows high out into the wind. Four seconds before I fall into the sea, three seconds, two seconds . . . We ought to create a sad and suspenseful mood like this and have the girls jump into the water one after another. Who could resist calling for us then? Finally someone picks up the phone to dial. The phone rings. But, alas! It's too late. These men are calling for me, but I've already dived into the deep, cold water. As if to mock their belated response, the white foam spreads out wide. And my body is nowhere to be found. At that moment, their hearts will break. And so, the girls will be released. But even if they are, does it mean that girls like us across the country will be set free? Am I right?

SE-MYŎNG: Next!

OK-JA: Excuse me, but I've got a problem. I'm awful sorry, but I can't go on television because of my mom. She'd kill herself if she saw me on TV like this. Oh, my mother! Can't we do this on the radio?

SE-MYŎNG: Wear this and go.

(He gives OK-JA his amusement-park mask. SE-MYŎNG carries a plastic barrel filled with gasoline from the engine room to the bow. The sound of a helicopter roars in the night sky.)

SE-MYŎNG: Here come the reporters! Get dressed, everybody!

KU-JA: Wow, it's the Kolean Bloadcasting System![6]

CH'UN-JA: Oh, no! It's MBC.

OK-JA: No, it's Traffic Control!

KIL-JA: You need a new pair of glasses. It's the Christian Broadcasting Network!

(SE-MYŎNG *shouts into the wireless radio, which he takes from the* STEERSMAN.)

SE-MYŎNG: Don't come any closer! Keep circling in the sky! I've got three barrels of gasoline here. If you come any closer, I'll set the boat on fire. Have your camera follow me. Follow me! (SE-MYŎNG *squeezes himself against the girls who have gathered as if posing for a picture.*) Everybody's got to remember the story of the rat, the story that was told to the king who loved fables. The story goes like this. A rat runs from a barn and plunges into the ocean at night. A second rat follows the first one and also jumps into the ocean at night. Then a third rat dives in. You must've guessed where this story is going already. Yes! The boxes you see here have forty-six girls in them. These girls, who could be your own daughters, are seventeen, eighteen, nineteen, twenty, and twenty-one years old. They're waiting to be sold to the small islands in the West Sea. These girls have taken an oath—like this.

KU-JA: (*Reading the pledge with difficulty due to her lack of education.*) "Covenant. If there's a generous person who is willing to pay off my debts, I'll be eternally grateful to that person. It'll make me believe that this world has not forsaken me. In order to pay back this gratitude, I'll live a normal life, having kids like my friend Sun-ae back home. But if no one cares about me, I'll say farewell to this world. I'll accept it as my fate that I was born under an unlucky star. September 1991.[7] Looking forward to the day of the full moon, sincerely, Hŏ Ku-ja." Here's my fingerprints instead of a signature. (*Hands over a bundle of forty-six written pledges to* SE-MYŎNG.)

SE-MYŎNG: Like fishermen on the shrimp boats, these girls will never get out of the islands alive. They've taken an oath to kill themselves by jumping into the water rather than go there. All forty-six girls have taken the pledge—without exception. In the old days, they called this "a noble death." *(Throws the bundle of pledges into the air.)* We'll start receiving your calls beginning now. You have thirty seconds. If there's no phone call, these beautiful young flowers will be buried deep in the sea. Get ready!

*(*MYŎNG CH'UN-JA *stands on the bow. She gleams with the expectation of going home. She is already visualizing her hometown, the village square, the blue moss growing around the well, and the wide dropwort field.)*

CH'UN-JA: Mother! It's Ch'un-ja. How've you been? I heard my aunt from Kalmŏri passed away. I got the news, but I couldn't get away because I had to work the nightshift at the factory. Whenever something important happens at home, I always have to work the damn nightshift. The timing's always bad.

(The ticks of the second hand of a watch abruptly stop. For a moment, all the characters hold their breath. The phone does not ring. Shadows fall over their disappointed faces. SE-MYŎNG *yanks the board on which* CH'UN-JA *stands.* CH'UN-JA *disappears into the sea. We hear her last cry, "Mother!" after she has disappeared.)*

SE-MYŎNG: Next!

YANG ŬN-SIL: *(Singing a popular song instead of making a last statement.)* "I want to bury my face in your arms today and cry. After all these years, our love remains only in my tears." Well, I don't think I have many years to live anyway. *(Plunges into the water.)*

SE-MYŎNG: Next!

PAK CHŎNG-SUN: *(Sings the Korean national anthem.)*

> *Until the East Sea's waves are dry, and Paek-tu-san worn away,*
> *God watch o'er our land forever! Our Korea Manse!*
> *Rose of Sharon, thousand miles of range and river land!*
> *Guarded by her people, ever may Korea stand!*
>
> *Like that south mountain armoured pine,—*

Would you make that call for me, please?—

> *standing on duty still,*
> *Wind or frost, unchanging ever, be our resolute will,*
> *In autumn's arching evening sky, crystal, and cloudless blue,*
> *Be the radiant moon our spirit, steadfast, single, and true.*
>
> *With such a will, such a spirit, loyalty, heart and hand,*
> *Let us love, come grief, come gladness, this, our beloved land!*[8]

(CHŎNG-SUN *dies.*)

SE-MYŎNG: Next! (SŎN-JA *almost faints from crying violently.*)

KIL-JA: Stop crying! I'll go.

(KIL-JA *steps onto the bow lighting a cigarette but immediately puts it out. She puts another cigarette in her mouth and then offers the pack around.*)

KIL-JA: I'm not here to sell cigarettes, you see. They won't hate me because I smoke, will they?

(*She starts to light a match but throws it away. Throws down the cigarette. Looks around. Strikes another match. In a daze, she brings the lit match to her lips, thinking she still has a cigarette in her mouth. Cries out that it's hot. She falls back and rolls down on the ground with her hands covering her face. She causes a huge commotion by shouting, writhing on the ground, and vomiting as if she were having an epileptic convulsion.* SE-MYŎNG *and the other girls try to calm her, but in vain. In the meantime,* SHIM CH'ŎNG *puts on* KIL-JA's *name tag* [*on which the amount of her debt is written*] *and then steps to the bow. Silence.*)

SHIM CH'ŎNG: (*Referring to* KIL-JA.) She'll go home. When someone calls, she'll go home, not me.

SE-MYŎNG: What if there's no call?

SHIM CH'ŎNG: It'll come.

SE-MYŎNG: But what if it doesn't?

SHIM CH'ŎNG: It will, it will. My name is Kil-ja. Twenty years old. Here I am looking for the moon hidden behind the clouds. I've taken off my shoes and put them over in the corner. Oh, dear moon, dear moon, I can't see in this darkness. Would you light my way?

SE-MYŎNG: (*Steps onto the bow behind* SHIM CH'ŎNG *and grabs her waist to drag her back down.)* Get down! It's not fair. You're cutting in ahead of others.

SHIM CH'ŎNG: Someone will call. I'll send her back home. What's wrong with that? Leave me alone.

(While they are struggling, the clock ticking stops. Silence. While standing on the plank, SE-MYŎNG *lifts up* SHIM CH'ŎNG *and places her on the bow, where she can pull out the plank with her hand. She pulls the plank and* SE-MYŎNG *disappears into the water, leaving a sharp cry behind him.* SHIM CH'ŎNG *steps out onto the bow by holding on to the railing of the ship. She kneels down and faces the television camera.)*

SHIM CH'ŎNG: Please give us a call, won't you? *(The* DRAGON KING *observes this.)*[9] Won't you keep your promise? The person who just . . . If you don't keep your promise—Wait, I've got an idea. *(She pulls her skirt up to cover her face and jumps into the ocean.)*

(All of the girls cry. The DRAGON KING *is incensed.)*

DRAGON KING: What're you girls making all this racket for? It means they died in vain. Just keep up what you've been doing. Don't you understand the wishes of the dead? There's still hope! Look! What do you see over there? That's the Cape of Hope, the mountain of our homeland. Let's row the boat toward it. Let's go home. Don't worry. We'll start to get phone calls right after we sacrifice about ten of you. Come on, let's go. Hey, Shim Ch'ŏng! Let me go with you. Wait a second! Hey, baby! I'm coming! Oops! It's cold! *(Disappears.)*

KIL-JA: Hurray! Hey, I quit this press conference. Cut it out, will you? I'm going back to Kunsan. Stop this nonsense, you bastards! Stop killing people. You butchers! Take away the camera! You! Do you wanna die?

KU-JA: Kil-ja, stop it. They say there's hope. Somebody will call. Didn't you hear the old man? The Cape of Hope is right over there. That's right. Look at them—they've been sacrificing themselves for us. We can't just sit here doing nothing. We've got to respond to their noble sacrifice. Come on! Let's keep going! Someone will call as long as we keep hope alive. Who's

next? Come out here. Show them. What are you hoping for?
(OK-JA *steps onto the bow wearing the helmet-mask she received from* SE-
MYŎNG. *The clock stops ticking.*)

KU-JA: What're you wearing? You need to take it off.

OK-JA: I'm afraid my mom will see my face.

KU-JA: Take it off. You've got to show your face to get calls.

(KU-JA *takes the mask off* OK-JA, *revealing the latter's bleeding face. One sees
a deep cut on her forehead. Blood streams from the cut, covering her whole
face, as though blood were being pumped from her eyes, nose, and mouth.
While* KU-JA *and her friends remain in a state of shock,* OK-JA *voluntarily
jumps into the water by kicking away the wood plank under her feet.*)

EVERYONE: Ok-ja! (*They run toward* OK-JA *to stop her, but in vain. Silence.
Someone cries out.*) It's a noble death!

(*All of the girls run toward the bow, shouting the same cry, "A noble death!"
They pull up their skirts to cover their faces, preparing to drown themselves.
The phone rings at this moment. Brief tableau.*)

VOICE: I am calling from Chŏngsŏn in Kangwon Province. Can I
join you there? My name's Yang Sun-dan. I'm fourteen years
old, going on fifteen. My debt isn't much. It's only a thousand.

(*The girls pull their skirts over their faces in readiness to jump into the water.
Everyone freezes as in an old, faded photograph.*)

NOTES

---

1. *I heard of a woman who makes big money selling tear gas* refers to the owner of a
   famous chemical company in Korea that produces tear-gas bombs.

2. *Yun Pong-gil* was a well-known fighter in Korea's independence move-
   ment against Japan. In 1932 he exploded a bomb in the midst of a Japanese
   war victory ceremony in Shanghai that was being held in conjunction
   with the Japanese emperor's birthday. The bomb killed or wounded several Japanese generals and officials. Yun was captured at the scene, tried
   by a military court in Osaka, and executed at the age of twenty-four.

3. *The tallest building in Seoul.* The Tower Building in Seoul, sixty-three stories
   high.

4. *Fabre.* French entomologist Jean-Henri Fabre (1823–1915).

5. *As I take off my shoes and put them in the corner to get ready to jump overboard.* These are old-fashioned rubber shoes that Korean women routinely left on a riverbank or beach when they committed suicide by drowning.

6. *Kolean Bloadcasting System.* In the original, Ku-ja mispronounces the English words for the Korean Broadcasting System. In the next speech, Ch'un-ja says "MC," omitting one of the English letters of the acronym, MBC (Moonhwa Broadcasting Company).

7. *September 1991.* In revivals of the play, Oh changed this reference to the month of the performance.

8. *Korean national anthem,* translated by John T. Underwood.

9. *(The DRAGON KING observes this.)* Spectators accustomed to realism may be surprised at this reappearance of the Dragon King, but he is a mythical character whose return reminds modern Koreans that traditional ways of thinking cannot be totally suppressed.

"The White Mask, the Moving Human Target!"

Each time a ball hits Se-myŏng, he shouts, "My future's bright! I'll make enough money to buy cows!"

"When your face appears on television, tell the viewers how much you owe your pimp as of today. Then somebody watching will pity you and promise to pay off your debts and save you." Se-myŏng counts the seconds while one of the girls waits for the call.

As the thirty seconds quickly tick away, each girl awaits a phone call from "a generous person" who will pay off her debts.

SELECTED BIBLIOGRAPHY

THE NUMBER OF studies in English on modern Korean drama and theater is small, although a recent increase in doctoral dissertations on these subjects bodes well for future publication. Listed below are some of the few studies available, together with a sampling of works on, and translations of, the theatrical and narrative sources of Oh T'ae-sŏk's plays.

Brandon, James R. *The Cambridge Guide to Asian Theatre*. New York: Cambridge University Press, 1993.

Cho, Oh-kon. "Korea." In *The Cambridge Guide to Theatre*, ed. Martin Banham. New York: Cambridge University Press, 1995.

—————. *Traditional Korean Theatre, Translated with the Introductions*. Berkeley: Asian Humanities Press, 1988.

Choi, Chungmoo. "Transnational Capitalism, National Imaginary, and the Protest Theater in South Korea." *Boundary 2: An International Journal of Literature and Culture* 22, no. 1 (1995): 235–261.

Erven, Eugene van. "Resistance Theatre in South Korea: Above and Underground." *TDR* 32, no. 3 (1988): 156–173.

Haboush, JaHyun Kim. *A Heritage of Kings: One Man's Monarchy in the Confucian World*. New York: Columbia University Press, 1988.

—————. *The Memoirs of Lady Hyegyong: The Autobiographical Writings of a Crown Princess of Eighteenth-Century Korea*. Berkeley: University of California Press, 1996.

Kardoss, John. *An Outline History of Korean Drama*. Greenville, N.Y.: Long Island University Press, 1966.

Kendall, Laurel. *Shamans, Housewives, and Other Restless Spirits: Women in Korean Ritual Life*. Honolulu: University of Hawai'i Press, 1985.

Khaznàdar, Cherif. "Korea's Masked Dances." *TDR* 26, no. 4 (1982), 64-65.

King, Eleanor. "The Holy-Unholy Shamans." *Korean Culture* 4, no. 4 (1983): 4–16.

Kister, Daniel A. "The Comic Vision of a Korean Shamanist Performance." In *Proceedings of the XIIIth Congress of the International Comparative Literature Association,* ed. Earl Miner, pp. 68–74. Tokyo: International Comparative Literature Association, 1995.

———. "Humor and Comedy in the World of the Kori-kut." *Korea Journal* 27, no. 5 (1987): 4–23.

———. "Korean Shamanist Theater and Drama." *Comparative Drama* 17, no. 2 (1983): 153–182.

Kloslova, Zdenka. "The Beginnings of the Modern Theatre in Korea." *Archiv Orientalni: Quarterly Journal of African, Asian, and Latin-American Studies* 57, no. 1 (1989): 47–56.

Korean Center of the International Theatre Institute. *The Korean Theater: Past and Present.* Seoul: ITI, 1981.

———. *The Korean Theater in 1991.* Seoul, ITI, 1991.

———. *The Korean Theater in 1992.* Seoul, ITI, 1992.

Korean National Commission for UNESCO. *Traditional Performing Arts of Korea.* Seoul: UNESCO, 1975.

———. *Wedding Day and Other Korean Plays.* Seoul: Shi-sa-yong-o-sa, 1983.

Kulikowski, Stanley. "Light/Liquid/Mist in Korea." *TDR* 24, no. 4 (1980): 115–118.

Lee, Meewon. "Shamanism and Korean Theatre." *Australasian Drama Studies* 27 (1995): 19–22.

Pihl, Marshall R. *The Korean Singer of Tales.* Cambridge, Mass.: Council on East Asian Studies, 1994.

Renouf, Renee, "Welcome to the Masquerade." *Korean Culture* 2, no. 4 (1982): 2–7.

Rhie, Sang-il. "Kabuki in Korea," trans. S. Han. *Asian Theatre Journal* 7, no. 1 (1990): 105–107.

Shim, Jung Soon. "The Image of Women in the Plays of Kim Cha-rim. *Korean Culture* 11, no. 2 (1990): 32–37.

Shin, Chong-ok. "The Reception of British-American Dramas and Its Influence on Modern Theatre." *Korea Journal* 28, no. 4 (1988): 20–33.

Suh, Yon-ho. "Status and Prospects of Korean Political Drama," trans. K. Ch'ae. *Korea Journal* 29, no. 8 (1989): 19–30.

Van Leest, Hyung-a Kim. "Political Satire in Yangju Pyolsandae Mask Drama." *Korea Journal* 31, no. 1 (1991): 87–109.

Walraven, Boudewijn. *Songs of the Shaman: The Ritual Chants of the Korean Mudang.* London: Kegan Paul, 1994.